Lungeing, Long-R
and
In-Hand Schooling

Lungeing, Long-Reining and In-Hand Schooling

CLAIRE LILLEY

J.A. ALLEN · LONDON

Dedication

This book is dedicated to 'The Boys' and Amadeus –
a very special horse who is never forgotten.

First published in 2015 by
J.A. Allen
Clerkenwell House
Clerkenwell Green
London EC1R 0HT
www.allenbooks.co.uk

J.A. Allen is an imprint of Robert Hale Limited

ISBN 978-1-908809-26-1

A catalogue record for this book is available from the British Library

Edited by Martin Diggle
Designed and typeset by Paul Saunders
Photographs by Dougald Ballardie
Diagrams by Carole Vincer

Printed in Singapore by Craft Print International Ltd

Contents

Acknowledgements

I would like to thank Lesley Gowers of J.A. Allen for giving me the opportunity to write this book. I have had it in mind for several years, and am thrilled that it has finally come to fruition. Thank you to Martin Diggle for being on my wavelength throughout the editing process, and to Carole Vincer for turning my rough drawings into the clear diagrams to illustrate the exercises. My husband has, as always, been brilliant at taking photographs with meaning. It is so difficult to capture the exact moment to go with what I am attempting to say, but I hope you will understand what I am trying to put across throughout this book. I am also very grateful to my friend Lorraine Mahoney for allowing me to use her and her horse Merlin for some of the photos.

And finally, a big thank-you to 'The Boys' – Heinrich, Norman and Mr Foley who teach me something new every day, and bring me to ever-increasing levels of self-awareness, which is an essential part of training horses.

The Horses

THE HORSES WHO appear most frequently in the photos used to illustrate this book are three of my own: Mr Foley (a 3-year-old Dutch x Thoroughbred gelding, real name Spartan Revelation), Heinrich (a 15-year-old Trakehner gelding, real name Broomdowns Donaupasquale) and Norman (a 12-year-old Hanoverian x Thoroughbred gelding, real name Dangerous Liaison). Amadeus, who also makes an appearance, was my Lippizaner x Thoroughbred gelding, who was about 10 years old at the time of the photos. I bought Amadeus as a yearling having seen him parading around a field at the head of a herd of young warmbloods. Norman is the only one I have not started from very young – he came to me as a 7-year-old from a showing background and has undergone a huge transformation over the last couple of years. I have known Heinrich and Mr Foley from a few days old; they were both bred by my friend Lynne Balcombe of Broomdown Stud in Kent.

Introduction

THERE ARE MANY misconceptions about lungeing. It is not about trotting the horse endlessly around in small circles 'to take the edge off him' before getting on board. Nor is it about strapping him into 'an outline' with his chin on his chest until he 'gives in'.

The horse likes to move: movement is natural to him. Whether schooling the horse from the ground or from the saddle, training is about learning how to work in harmony with the horse, developing his mind and body to make him more beautiful and powerful.

Your horse should trust that you would not frighten or hurt him. You need to have faith that he will not forget you exist and mow you down if he gets spooked. It is your duty as a horse owner to care for the horse, and to look after his needs, taking into consideration his natural instincts of being a flight animal. He needs to be part of your 'herd' with you as 'herd leader'. This entails training the horse to understand his role. A happy horse is one who understands where he fits in, that he is cared for, fed and watered, and that he is appreciated and loved by you.

'Working from the ground' encompasses everything from developing trust and responsiveness to developing the right muscles needed for ridden work, and teaching the horse an understanding of the rein and whip aids. In fact, many ridden problems can be rectified from the ground. Riders so often battle on with their horses, their idea of a solution being to purchase a new saddle, a stronger bit, or treatment by this or that therapist, rather than spending time schooling their horse from the ground. Lungeing, in-hand work, and long-reining are invaluable when trying to get to the bottom of a ridden issue. Being on the ground allows the rider to observe how their horse behaves and moves without them. More often than not, groundwork

The horse is a flight animal by nature but, as well as running away from danger, will run free from sheer pleasure.

A good relationship with your horse is built on trust and confidence in each other. If you trust your horse, he will trust you. If you have confidence in his ability, he will have confidence in you as a rider and trainer.

During this period, the equipment used for the in-hand work was developed. Lunge cavessons in various forms, with nosebands made from leather or metal, were used to teach the horse to be submissive. The nose aids with the lunge rein attached to the cavesson could be stronger than those using the bit reins, to protect the sensitive mouth. Rollers may have been used for long-reining horses in preparation for draught work before they were taken up for groundwork in the dressage sphere, and it is likely that they were an adaptation of the 'saddle' or 'pad' used in draught work. Various auxiliary reins were also invented, one of which, the Chambon (named for its French inventor) is referred to within these pages, being a valuable schooling aid.

Horses also used to be attached to two pillars to train them for working 'on the spot' in the piaffe but, on my last visit to The Spanish Riding School, this was no longer part of the show programme. However, public performances of both ridden and in-hand work by The Spanish Riding School, and others that follow the classical tradition, such as The Cadre Noir in France, the Royal Andalusian School of Equestrian Art and The Portuguese School of Equestrian Art can be seen to this day, and are well worth a visit.

The importance of groundwork today

Lungeing, long-reining and in-hand work remain very relevant to today's equestrian sports.

In dressage, is it not better to educate the horse, and the rider, on the ground initially? A novice horse with sound basic training on the lunge to will be easier to ride and have every chance of progressing to the higher levels than one who has no muscular strength and poor concentration.

Dressage is the foundation training for all other equestrian sports; it is about the skill of using the seat, leg and rein aids (using a bit) as a whole as well as developing a true partnership with the horse. Issues that arise when riding, which often result in the rider using a stronger bit, a different noseband, giving different feed and so on, can so often be avoided by intelligent training from the ground.

Dressage is the foundation for all equestrian sports. A novice horse with sound basic training on the lunge to will be easier to ride and have every chance of progressing to the higher levels.

It takes may years of patient training, both from the ground as well as in the saddle, to achieve success at Grand Prix level in dressage.

Below Harmony between horses and their riders. If the horse has confidence in his rider from the ground, he will happily cope with all situations. These Andalusians are all aware of each other – note their ears are alert to their teammates, but they are also obedient to their riders.

Jumping on the lunge in the school, or tackling obstacles in the field or on the cross-country course, can be extremely useful for building the horse's confidence. The horse's speed and line of approach can be controlled from the ground. The person lungeing can assess the horse's natural jumping ability, and can improve his athleticism and technique and teach the horse to think for himself, which can be a life-saver under saddle where the horse can save the situation and get the rider out of trouble.

In addition to benefiting what are often, nowadays, considered the main equestrian sports of dressage, showjumping and eventing, groundwork remains of great value in other areas. Lungeing and long-reining

Right Competing at the highest level in showjumping. Horse and rider have total confidence in each other.

Below Eventing requires a real partnership between horse and rider to reach top level. This is not achieved by riding alone – all aspects of the horse's care and training, including groundwork, play a very important part in being the very best.

are part and parcel of preparing a horse to pull a vehicle. Driving horses have to be able to react instantly to their driver's aids. The risk of a nasty accident can be prevented by spending time on responsiveness and clarity of the aids.

The sport of vaulting requires a very special horse – one who can maintain a faultless rhythm on the lunge and be happy to work on the left rein (the rein normally used for this discipline) for prolonged periods. However, it goes without saying that horses used for vaulting must be schooled on both reins to keep them fit and supple and to prevent crookedness. They must also

An example of great control – driving horses warming up, working on long-reins in close proximity.

Below Carriage driving a four-in-hand in the dressage phase of a competition.

A team of four horses tackle the marathon course – a feat of great skill, requiring quick reactions from both driver and horses, and a huge amount of trust.

be totally unfazed by the gymnastics taking place on their backs, so developing calmness is a major part of the groundwork process.

In showing classes, unless your horse or pony can stand impeccably still for the judge, you will undoubtedly lose marks, and obedience in hand is essential during the trot-up.

It is also the case that different aspects of groundwork can benefit each other. For example, lungeing a horse can be done in a school, a round pen, field – anywhere that has a safe, level surface. Confining lunge work to a designated small area or a round pen limits the possibilities of variation. The high fence of a pen may be useful if working the horse 'free', of if the horse has issues and is likely to jump out, but most people do not have such an enclosed area and, in any case, repeating the same-sized circle over and over again is bound to cause muscle strain and boredom. For this reason, I personally prefer to lunge in a conventional rectangular school, which gives me the option of working the horse in different patterns – on straight

Above The vaulting horse must be extremely calm on the lunge, able to maintain a steady rhythm at canter, and totally unfazed by what is happening on his back at all times.

Right Standing still for inspection at a show. It is so important to teach your horse to remain calm in halt for a long time.

lines as well as different-sized circles, so training can be imaginative and varied, giving the horse a good gymnastic workout. However, if a horse is acting up and continually 'gets away' in such a situation, then in-hand work and/or long-reining can be useful to correct the problems before attempting to lunge again.

Leading in hand at a showing class.

Working the horse on long-reins in the field adds variety to schooling.

CHAPTER ONE

Equipment

IN THIS CHAPTER, I will look at the various items necessary for the different types of groundwork.

For the horse

Roller or saddle and girth

A roller or saddle is needed if you are working your horse in a piece of equipment that needs attaching to a girth.

A roller is ideal, as you can see the horse's back muscles working (or not!) as he moves. A choice of roller rings at different heights is an advantage so that side-reins etc. can be attached at exactly the correct height for the individual horse. A roller pad will make for a cosy fit behind the withers, especially if your roller is not padded either side of the withers, which raises the roller slightly off the spine.

Lungeing in a saddle is fine if you are working from the ground as a preparation for riding. If you are using a saddle, it must fit well enough so that it does not slip forwards, or off to one side when the horse is moving. The girth must be secure enough to keep the saddle in place, especially if your horse is likely to play around. However, for the sensitive horse, or ticklish types, or youngsters being introduced to the girth for the first time, comfort is paramount. A soft, padded, or elasticated girth is useful here: don't use the tough old leather girth that you found mouldering away in the corner of the tack room, because it will be stiff, and will rub the sensitive skin behind the elbows. Also, although the girth must be tight enough to do its job, it is

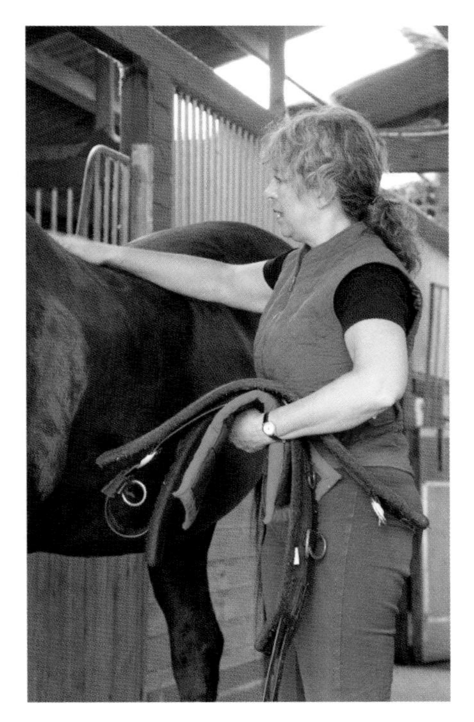

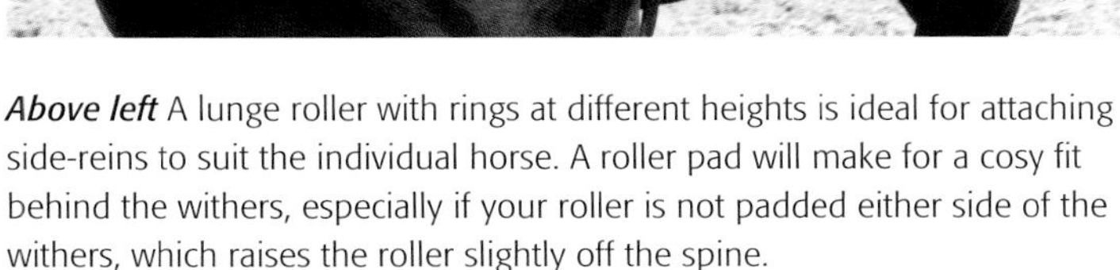

Above left A lunge roller with rings at different heights is ideal for attaching side-reins to suit the individual horse. A roller pad will make for a cosy fit behind the withers, especially if your roller is not padded either side of the withers, which raises the roller slightly off the spine.

Above right Put the roller on by folding the girth on the top, placing the roller on the horse's back, and lowering the girth on the offside before fastening it on the nearside in the same way as you would put a saddle on.

important not to over-tighten it. If you do this, and/or do it up too suddenly, you can frighten your horse, and end up with a 'girth-shy' horse who will put his ears back as soon as he sees you approaching with his tack.

Running the stirrups up with the stirrup leathers wrapped around the irons prevents the saddle from being scratched as the stirrups bounce on the saddle. Alternatively, you could lunge with the stirrups down. Personally I prefer to do the latter, as the irons do not then thump against the saddle noisily, which can alarm some horses. Also, letting the stirrups hang gets a young horse used to them, and prepares him for accepting the rider's legs against his sides. They do not move around as much as you would expect!

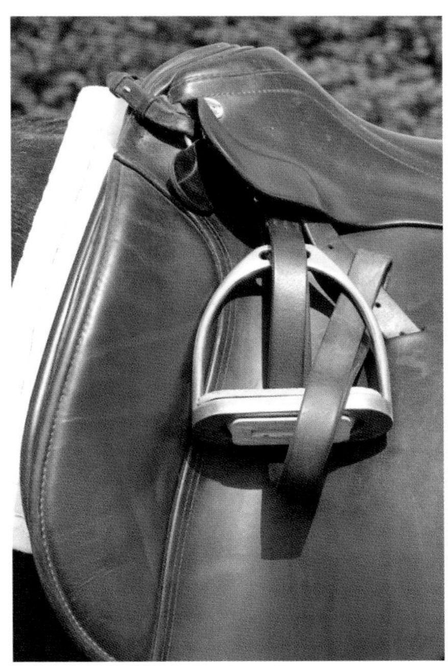

Running the stirrups up with the stirrup leather wrapped around the iron prevents the saddle from being scratched as the stirrups bounce on the saddle.

Side-reins etc. can be attached to the girth. There are different ways of doing this. One way is to pass each side-rein under the front girth strap, around the rear girth strap, and back under the front one again before doing up the buckle. This prevents the side-rein from slipping down, which is useful if your horse tends to pull down into the contact.

If your horse is able to work in self-carriage, and is not 'rude' with the contact, then you can simply fasten the side-reins around the first girth straps. This prevents the saddle being pulled forwards, which can happen if you do the side-reins up around both girth straps. Alternatively, you can purchase a pair of detachable 'side-rein rings' that slide on to both girth straps. These are very useful for long-reining also, as there is no need to pass the long-reins through the stirrups. (A lot of people avoid long-reining for the reason that they are awkward to attach. It is common to tie the stirrups to each other with baler twine, passing it under the horse's stomach, which in itself can be a tricky move! A single long-rein, which clips on to the girth buckles or side-rein rings attached to the girth – as above – is far easier than two separate lunge reins. Using two lunge reins means that you have an awful lot of spare in your hands, which is easy to drop, or to get tangled around your legs, let alone the horse's!)

Below left One way of fastening side-reins to the girth is to pass each side-rein under the front girth strap, around the rear girth strap, and back under the front one again before doing up the buckle. This prevents the side-rein from slipping down, which is useful if your horse tends to pull down into the contact.

Below right Side-rein rings (one each side of the saddle), which slide on to the girth straps, are a useful way of attaching side-reins to the girth.

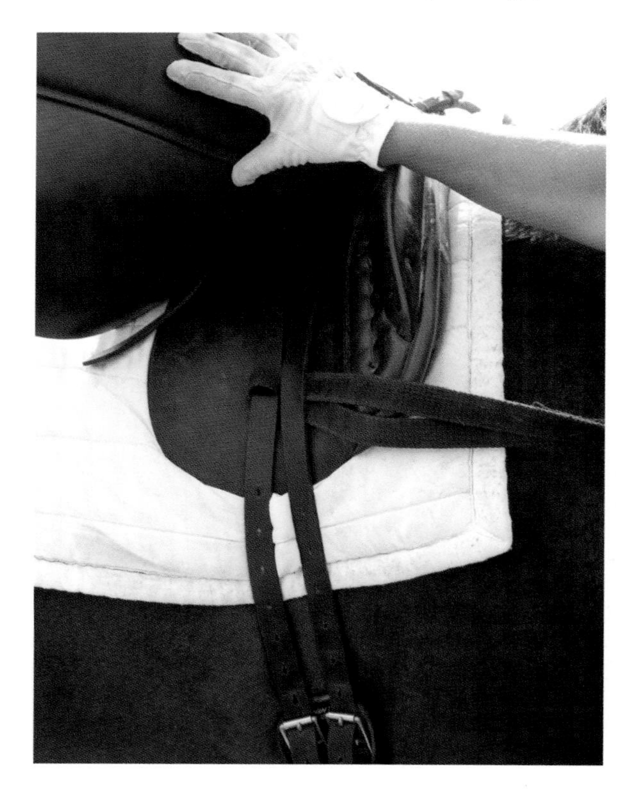

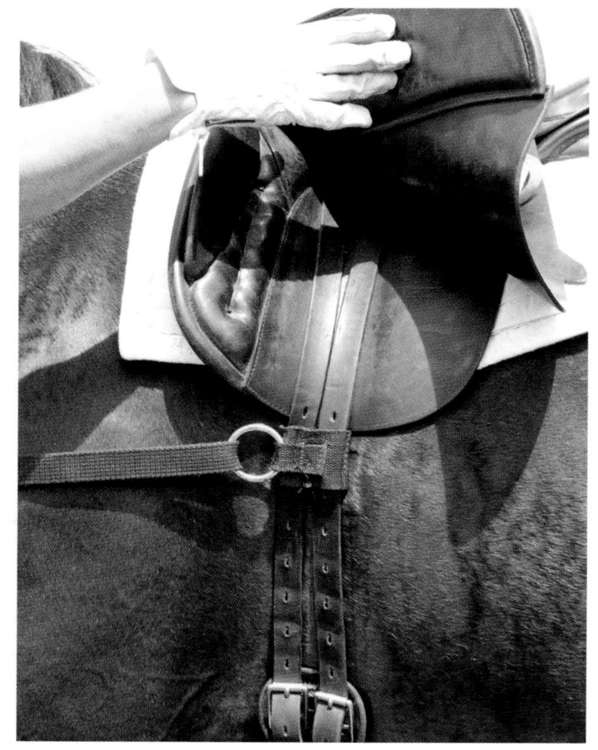

Lunge cavesson

A well-fitting lunge cavesson is extremely useful. A lunge rein, or long-reins, come to that, can all be attached to the rings on the noseband of a lunge cavesson. Some lunge cavessons facilitate the attachment of a bit to the cheekpieces, which dispenses the need for using both a bridle and a cavesson together. This is ideal, as there is not too much clutter on the horse's head. If you are using a lunge cavesson over the bridle, it is possible to do away with the noseband on the bridle, but if your horse has a tendency to open his mouth to avoid bit pressure, or gets his tongue over the bit, you may need to use a noseband. A drop noseband is best as it will not be under the cavesson nosepiece. If you do not have a lunge cavesson, then a bit connector fastened to the front of a drop noseband works very well. If your horse is

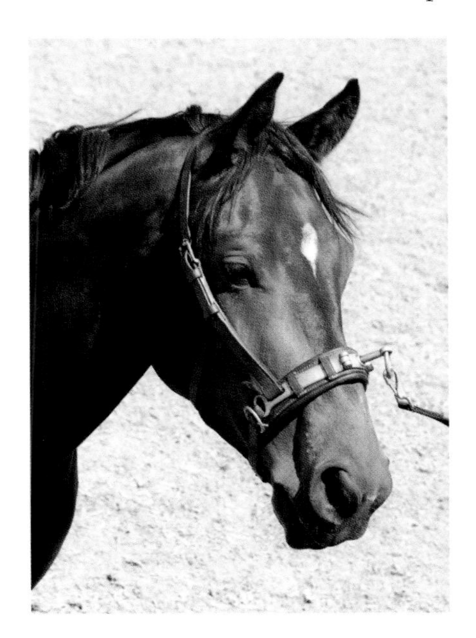

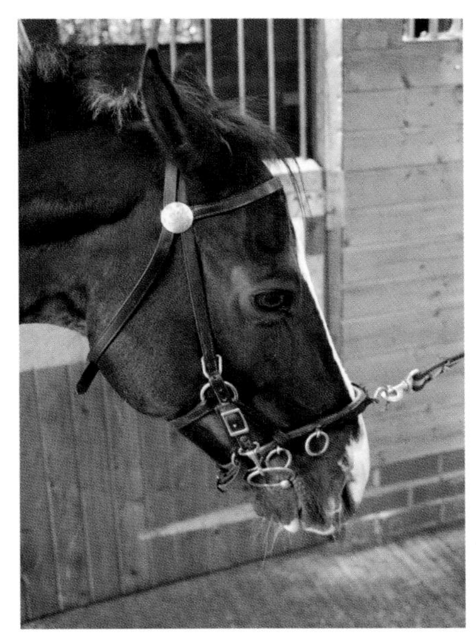

Above left A well-fitting leather lunge cavesson.

Above right A lunge cavesson with cheekpieces allowing a bit to be attached directly to the cavesson does away with needing to use a bridle under the lunge cavesson.

RIght If you do not have a lunge cavesson, then a bit connector fastened to the front of a drop noseband works very well.

not happy with nose pressure, a bit connector under the chin helps to keep the bit level and prevents it from being pulled to one side of the mouth. That said, you should not be pulling anyway!

Bridle

The horse can be worked in hand from a bridle, lunge cavesson or a control halter. In the early stages of groundwork training, developing a relationship with your horse and establishing the basics of control and understanding can be done in a halter or headcollar, though a bit is necessary to teach your horse about 'contact' and working correctly through the back in a rounded outline. A simple bit such as a training snaffle with a lozenge in the middle is my personal favourite and it suits most horses. Make sure the bit is not too thick, which would be too much of a mouthful, nor too thin, which would be too sharp.

If your horse is not happy with nose pressure, a bit connector under the chin helps to keep the bit level and prevents it from being pulled to one side of the mouth.

There are many different ideas about how to attach the lunge rein to the bridle. Attaching the lunge rein to both the noseband and bit ring (see photo opposite) prevents the bit from sliding to one side of the horse's mouth. Passing the lunge rein through the inside bit ring, over the poll to the outside bit ring causes uneven, and unnecessary, poll pressure and causes the horse to twist his head to one side. Passing the lunge rein through the inside bit ring and fastening it to the outside ring tightens the bit against the corners of the horse's mouth and pinches his tongue. Attaching the lunge rein to the inside bit ring helps both the horse and the rider develop sensitivity to the rein contact. It also avoids the pinching action mentioned above.

If you are lungeing, it is best to take the reins off altogether, but if you are riding afterwards, twist the reins and pass the throatlash between them to secure the reins under the horse's throat out of the way.

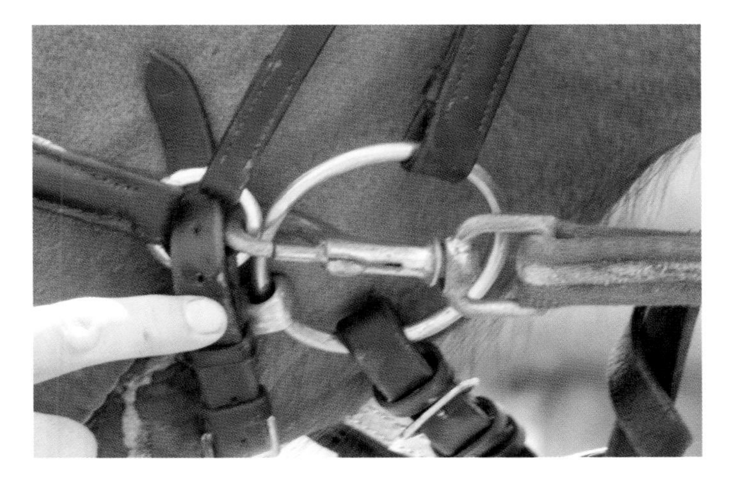

Above Correct: attaching the lunge rein to the noseband and bridle prevents the bit from sliding to one side of the horse's mouth.

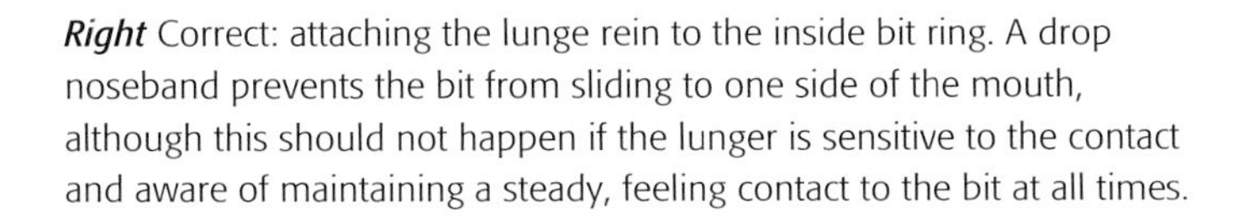

Right Correct: attaching the lunge rein to the inside bit ring. A drop noseband prevents the bit from sliding to one side of the mouth, although this should not happen if the lunger is sensitive to the contact and aware of maintaining a steady, feeling contact to the bit at all times.

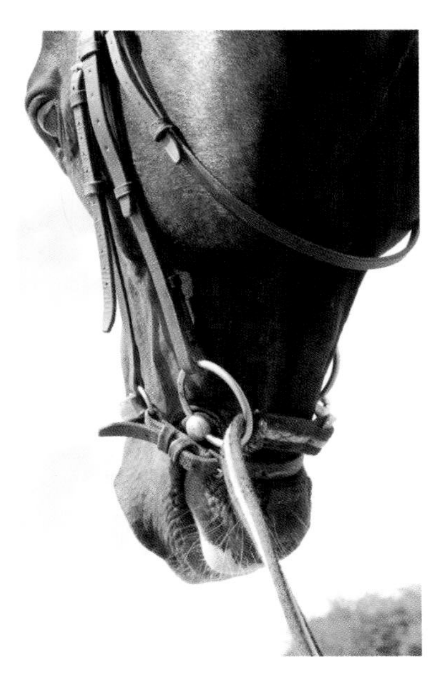

Left and centre Wrong: passing the lunge rein through the inside bit ring, over the poll to the outside bit ring causes uneven, and unnecessary, poll pressure and causes the horse to twist his head to one side. Also, any pressure from the lunger pulls the bridle crooked. ***Above*** Wrong: passing the lunge rein through the inside bit ring, under the chin, and fastening it to the outside bit ring tightens the bit against the corner of the horse's mouth.

It is far safer to deal with a horse who has little or no respect for the bit from the ground than it is to try to ride through issues on board. So many accidents happen because the horse does not understand the rider's aids. The rider pulls on the reins in an effort to stop the horse: the horse pulls against the rider. The rider resorts to a stronger bit, or draw reins. The horse either fights more, or becomes 'helpless', shutting down mentally as a defence against the rider. If the rider takes time to learn about how rein contact should feel from the ground, these unpleasant situations can be avoided. Both horse and rider learn the value of mutual respect, trust and sensitivity. From this foundation, their partnership will be vastly improved and a pleasure rather than a nightmare.

The Be-Nice halter, which is very useful for loading, lungeing and in-hand work without a bit in the early stages of training, or with horses who have contact issues with the mouth.

Training halter

There are various training halters available. The principle behind these is 'pressure, release'. If the horse pulls, the handler maintains the pressure on the lead rope, causing the halter to tighten around the horse's head. Once the horse stops pulling, to relieve the pressure on the rope, the handler slackens the rope. As the rope slackens, so does the halter. This a great way to teach the horse respect: if he misbehaves, pressure increases; if he behaves, the pressure ceases. (Good cop, bad cop.) A training halter can be used for handling, loading, in-hand work, and lungeing in the early stages, especially with a young horse who is not yet familiar with a bit. It is also useful for horses who have bitting issues, so they can learn to relax in their work before the bridle is reintroduced.

Leg protection

It is advisable to protect your horse's legs with boots or bandages. If your horse is well balanced, and working on a familiar surface that he is used to, you may feel you can do without. However, if you are lungeing on uneven ground, or in a school with a different surface from what your horse is used to, or in unfamiliar surroundings, or it is a blustery day and your horse is having a bit of a play around, then you would be advised to guard against leg injuries.

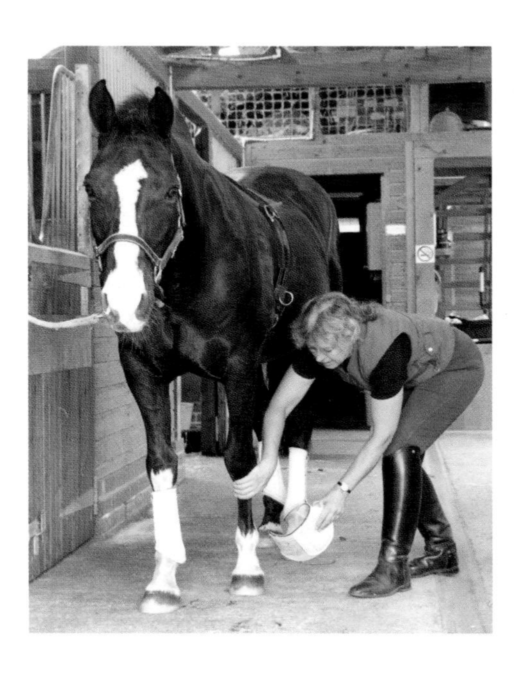

Left Putting on brushing boots. *Above* Ready to lunge.

For the handler

Lunge or lead rein

A lunge rein should be about 8m long, with a hand loop at one end for the trainer, and a swivel clip for attachment to the bit/lunge cavesson/training headcollar. It can be made from webbing, either padded or plain, from leather, either flat or rolled, or cord.

A lead rein for close-up in-hand work should be about 3m in length, and can be made from rope, webbing or leather, with a hand loop at one end and a swivel clip at the other.

When using a lunge rein or lead rein/rope, it is very important not to get it wrapped around your hand or wrist, just in case your horse pulls away: you must be able to let go, and not be caught up. If you do put your hand through the loop, just hold it across your fingers so you can release it easily. Alternatively, fold the rein in even loops across your hand.

Whip

A lunge whip is needed for lunge work where you are a distance from the horse. You should be close enough to the horse so that, if necessary, you can touch him with the end of the lash. To make a large circle (of radius bigger the than length of the lunge rein), you just need to walk a small circle yourself. You can then make the lungeing circle as big as required and still be able to touch the horse with your whip. This is important as, otherwise, a horse will soon becomes aware that he is 'out of range' of the whip and lose respect for the trainer. There is no point in smacking the ground with it (as many people do) because the horse does not learn what the touch of the whip means. Cracking the whip to make a noise rather than touching the horse has the disadvantage of teaching the horse to react to sudden noises – not a good idea if you want a confident horse who remains calm in noisy situations!

In case you are throwing your hands up in horror at the thought of using a whip, just remember it is an aid, not a punishment. Teaching the horse the touch of a whip from the ground will reap awards when ridden work is introduced. You will be able to carry a schooling whip with no problems if you have taught your horse to understand the whip from the ground.

For in-hand work, you could use either a long schooling whip, a driving whip with a lash, or a piaffe whip, with a short lash. Failing that, a lunge whip with the lash cut off at about 10cm works very well.

Using a whip correctly, whether it is a lunge whip, driving or piaffe whip, or a schooling whip, is totally dependent on body language (see below) and presence of mind. It should *never* be used in anger. Think of a whip as an arm extension, so you can touch the horse without being in the firing line of the teeth or the hooves. The whip aid is a substitute for your leg aid when schooling from the ground, and is a necessary 'body aid', as is the lunge or lead rein. You need a connection to the horse. One day, when you have a close bond with your horse, he will listen to your every tiny gesture – the pointing of a finger, a movement of your feet, for instance. But in the early stages you will need all the aids you have at your disposal, as well as being quick-thinking, with clear reactions to those of your horse. Any dithering about will confuse him.

Protective clothing

Riding hat/helmet

A protective helmet is advisable when working horses from the ground. Just because you are not riding your horse, do not assume you will not get hurt. A head-butt from a horse can knock you off your feet, and you may get trampled. This may sound dramatic, but believe me it does happen. You need to keep your wits about you, and take care. (You also need to be fit and able to run like mad should you need to!)

Sensible footwear

It is all too easy to trip over, or be pushed off balance by the horse. Wear footwear that fits well, and is securely fastened, with no trailing laces. Since you may get your feet trodden on, soft wellingtons or trainers are to be avoided since they will give your toes no protection from wayward hooves! Stout walking boots are ideal. (If you do groundwork in riding boots, take any spurs off to avoid tripping over your own feet.)

Gloves

Gloves are essential – rope burns hurt! Gloves should fit your fingers well so you have a good grip and feel on the rein, but should be loose enough around the wrist that they will come off should you get a hand caught up in the rein.

Other 'equipment' for the handler

Here, I am referring not to mechanical equipment or items of clothing, but to important factors that equip the handler to communicate successfully with the horse.

Body language

Horses are highly sensitive to body language. Every twitch of a nostril, or flick of an ear means something. They are very perceptive to how we stand and move, how we breathe and how we think and feel. A horse will react adversely

Norman having a 'moment'. My body language is supportive – note the whip is low and an extension of my arm.

to a person who is fearful long before the person realizes it for themselves. A person who loves their horse will have a good relationship with him. If you do not like a horse, or even hate him, he will never give his best to you.

If you are going to train your horse successfully, you need all of the following positive feelings in bucket-loads:

Positive feelings. Think positive, and all will be well!

If your horse has a nervous disposition, or has 'baggage' from poor training/bad experiences in the past, it is imperative that you exude positive feelings to him constantly, to reassure him.

It is also important to feel good in yourself. Be happy, and maintain a positive energy throughout your body – a bit like having a force-field of power around you.

If the horse spooks or becomes afraid of something, keep working calmly with him, and he will very quickly get over it. Imagining it will all go horribly wrong is just a recipe for disaster!

See and feel what you want the horse to see and feel, and the outcome will be positive.

Anticipating a spook, or worrying about being trampled underfoot, will all transfer to the horse, who will pick up your anxiety. If you give the horse the chance of being afraid or misbehaving, he may well act upon it. Think positive, and all will be well! Think badly, and it will all go badly!

If you are having problems with your horse, take a long, hard look at yourself, and be totally honest. How many of the following negative feelings do you have?

Negative feelings. Think badly, and it will all go badly!

If you are frightened of your horse, admit it. If you do not like your horse, you will never get him to work for you. If you cannot deal with him, get professional help, or sell him. You may have personal issues that are affecting your relationship with your horse, in which case you may perhaps need professional help in the way of counselling. Horses can bring out the best in some people, and the worst in others. They teach us things about ourselves that we did not know. If your horse is misbehaving, try to understand why. Horses are not born bad, but can become downright dangerous with the wrong handling. Correcting a poorly trained horse takes time, and all the feelings on the 'positive' list. If you have anything from the 'negative' list, you will not succeed.

If you do not use your body's energy and cannot remain focused, your posture will suffer. A negative attitude causes you to slump – blocking your energy field – then you wonder why your horse is taking no notice of you. If your mind is wandering on to other thoughts outside what you are trying to achieve with your horse, he will not pick up on what you want him to do. Worrying about booking the car in for an overdue service, or why the kids are bunking off school means nothing to your horse – such worries just cloud your intuition and the clarity of thought that your horse needs from you. If he pulls away from you and runs off, just take a moment to refocus, and he will listen again.

Handler unsure, horse unsure. Here I am approaching my young horse, leaning forwards as I do so, and looking slightly tentative. 'What are you going to do? Are you going to stand still?' My 3-year-old Mr Foley's expression seems to say 'What are *you* going to do to *me*? Shall I run away?'

Here I am thinking, 'Good boy, I am not going to hurt you', and he is thinking, 'Oh good, she is telling me what to do. This is familiar, and I trust her.'

To work. I am thinking, 'Let's move sideways.' Note my low whip carriage next to Mr Foley, encouraging him to step sideways with me. We are working as a team. Mr Foley is chewing with his mouth; a sign of showing acceptance of what I am asking of him. From his expression, he is concentrating totally on me.

Voice aids

Using the right tone of voice at the right moment is essential when training your horse. Your voice goes hand-in-hand with your body language and feelings. Whether you are calm and confident, or stressed and angry, this will show in your voice. It takes a lot of practice to say nothing. Horses like peace and quiet. If you are constantly nagging him out of fear or frustration, your horse will become tense and agitated. Naughtiness is usually a result of fear, tension, or misunderstanding. Being calm and saying nothing can often diffuse a situation. Horses do learn to respond to words: in the same way that a dog learns how to 'sit' or to 'fetch', a horse will learn to 'stand', or to 'trot'. However, rather than having an intellectual understanding of what a word 'means', the horse makes an association with the sound, so in principle you could use any words you like – if you say 'sausages' as a command to mean 'stop', it will work as long as you *always* say 'sausages'! Thus it is important to be *consistent* with the words you use. The tone of voice is also fundamentally important. Voice aids can be commands, such as 'whoa' or 'no!' or they can be praise such as 'good boy' or 'super'. They can be calming, such as 'steady', or invigorating, such as 'come on'.

A horse who has been correctly trained to the trainer's voice, body language, contact with the rein and the touch of a whip will eventually learn to react to the pointing of a finger instead, or even small changes in the trainer's body language and mental focus. This is such a satisfying goal to achieve – being able to guide your horse without even touching him.

CHAPTER **TWO**

The Unbacked Horse

THERE IS NOTHING more pleasurable than handling an 'easy' horse. This goes without saying, I am sure, for every vet, saddler, dentist and instructor as well as every horse owner. Once the basic rules have been established, training in hand, on the lunge and long-reining can proceed.

Basic handling – manners and obedience

General good manners in the stable are paramount to a well-behaved horse. The horse needs to learn good behaviour in all situations, and anywhere. This takes time, and requires an owner who recognizes when their horse is afraid, or when he does not understand what is required of him. Certainly, horses can become naughty and defensive if their trainer has no empathy, and they can become belligerent if their owner is too soft with them and lets them get away with misbehaving.

Biting and kicking are natural reactions for horses in the wild having a disagreement amongst themselves. This can be seen, in particular, amongst young stallions attempting to stamp their authority on each other. Horses do, then, 'play rough'. Mostly they just threaten to 'duff each other up', but they can really hurt each other if they want to. In such a mode your horse may kick out at you, 'defending' his territory in his stable or field, or he may charge at you with his teeth bared, or rear up, waving his front hooves in your direction, which may be his way of wanting to 'play'. Even if your horse gives you a friendly head-butt you may end up with concussion! Such actions must be tempered for your own safety. Your horse must learn that a human is not a horse and this behaviour is absolutely not allowed. This comes down to your body language, attitude and confidence.

Above left Your young horse may try to intimidate you, but it important that he learns that this behaviour is not acceptable. Your body language is very important, and you must be 'the boss'.

Above right A few moments later. My body language is friendly and relaxed, and young Mr Foley has lowered his neck and calmed down.

Left A few minutes free in the school can relieve any underlying tension.

Too much 'coochy-cooing' can turn your horse into a spoilt brat in no time at all, and he will walk all over you – literally. Barging is a sign that your horse reckons that he, not you, is 'herd leader'. It only takes a couple of instances in which the horse is not reprimanded for poor behaviour for him to believe that he is 'the boss'. However, your reactions in disciplining the horse must be instant, in order that he makes the connection between his behaviour and your response. (This is equally true when you reward or praise good behaviour, which hopefully will be a more regular occurrence.) Note that mares will be pretty tough when disciplining their foals. They may kick or bite them, or give them a good shove, even knocking them to the ground. In making this point, I am not suggesting that you abuse your horse but, if you have a boisterous, bargy horse, giving him a good shove can work wonders. On a less dramatic note, it is worth remembering that horses are herd animals and one of the best ways to 'make your point' to a horse is to ignore him, effectively shunning him from your 'herd'. This can have a dramatic effect on a wilful animal.

Grooming and foot care

Grooming should be a pleasurable experience for the horse, but some, particularly colts, can be very ticklish. Take time over this, using a soft brush, or a stable rubber, or a grooming mitt for example. With very ticklish horses, just touching them with your hand will be as much as they can tolerate to start with, but do reprimand any biting or kicking. Reward the horse when he is calm and accepts your touch. Bear in mind that if you cannot touch your horse all over, how are you going to tack him up? Putting rugs on will also be an issue.

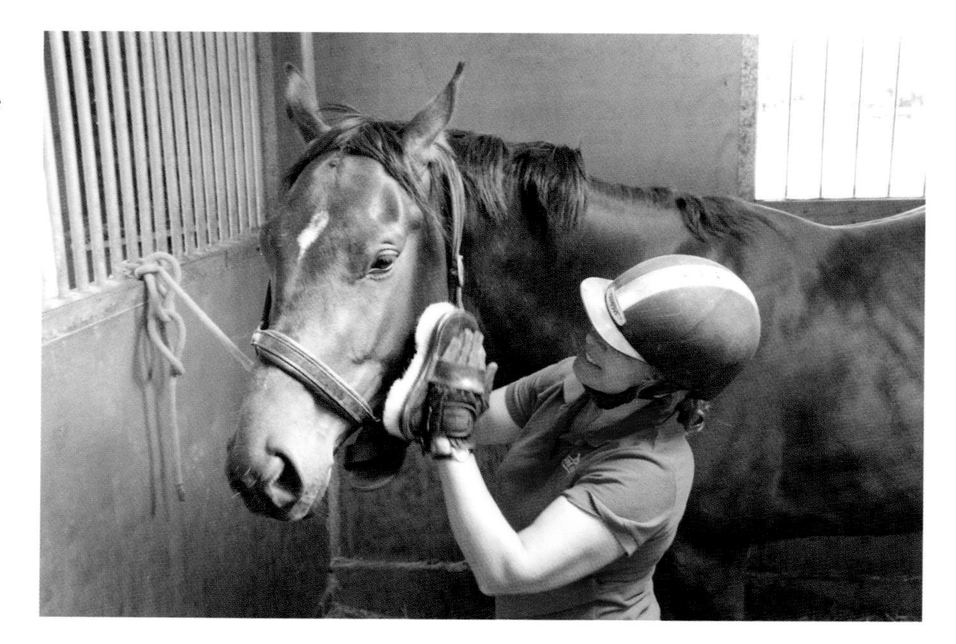

Grooming should be a pleasurable experience, but some colts are ticklish. Here Mr Foley is going through a ticklish phase, hence the expression on his face. He liked to sniff everything before it came anywhere near him at this stage.

Your horse's feet should be regularly trimmed and balanced by the farrier or barefoot trimmer. Shoeing should not be necessary until the horse begins ridden work, but even then, if you are not going on hard ground, your horse may not need shoes. However, it is important to train him to accept his feet being handled and picked out, to make both this process and the hoofcare professional's job as easy as possible. Once your horse has picked up the foot you have asked him to a few times, allow him to stand still and relax, praising him. If you have problems picking your horse's feet up in the stable, and he is trying to kick out at you, or flatten you against a wall, practise in the school, using a whip to touch his leg so you are out of harm's way

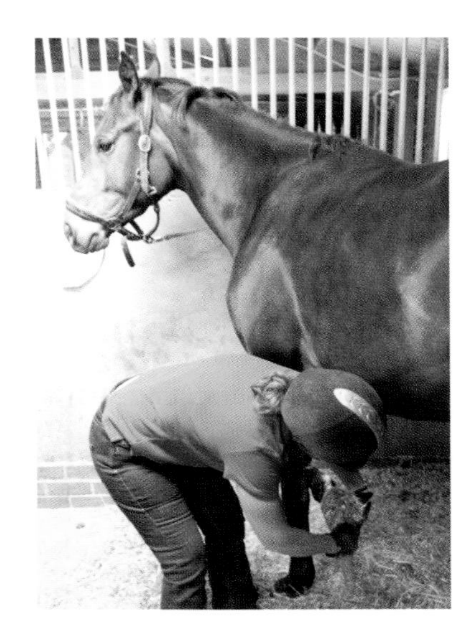

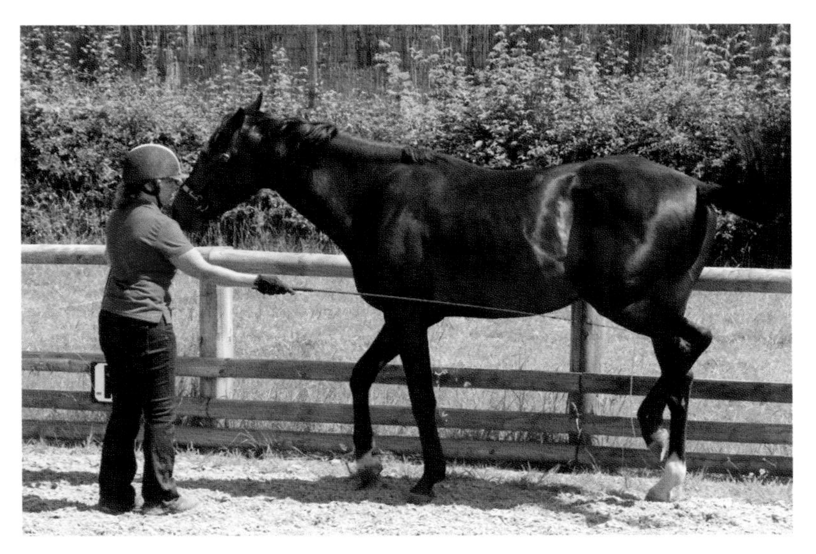

Above left Accepting having feet picked out is a lesson that needs to be learnt early on.

Above right If you have problems picking up your horse's feet in the stable, and he is trying to kick out at you, or flatten you against a wall, practise in the school, using a whip to touch his leg so you are out of harm's way.

Left Always praise your horse when he does well.

Introducing tack

Get him used to wearing all the tack you will need to train him from the ground, such as a roller, bridle, lunge cavesson and boots (boots are quicker to put on and take off a young horse than bandages). Putting things on and taking them off should be repeated many times – several times a day if possible, until he accepts everything calmly and confidently. Do it in short lessons of about ten minutes: for example, put the bridle on and take it off three times in the morning, do the same with the roller a few times later on in the day, then fit the front boots only on another lesson, then all four boots.

Let a horse touch new items with his nose and sniff them before fitting them for the first time. When introducing tack, be aware that, if the horse seems to have an issue with a particular item, there may be an underlying reason for this, other than him being simply 'awkward' – see Avoiding Misunderstandings at the end of this chapter.

Build up gradually over a few days to being able to tack him up as necessary for a training session in the school. He can be worked in whatever piece of equipment you have put on him. For example, if he is used to a training halter only, then you can do some simple groundwork and basic lungeing with him. When he accepts a roller, then he can be schooled using one.

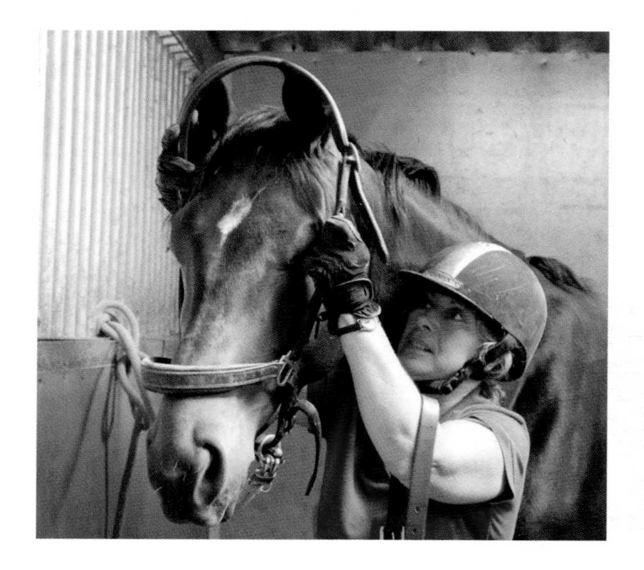

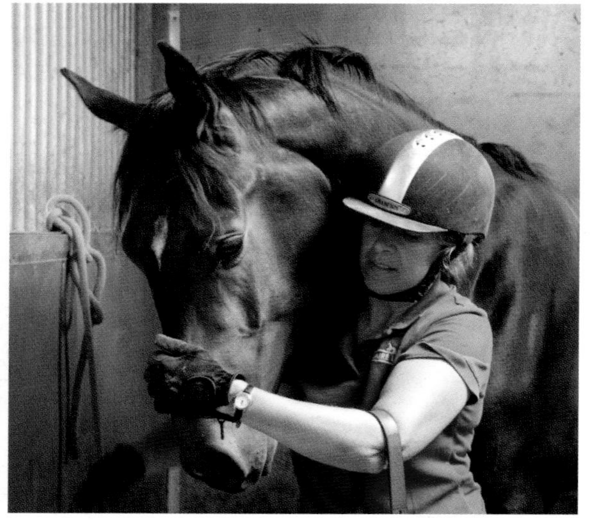

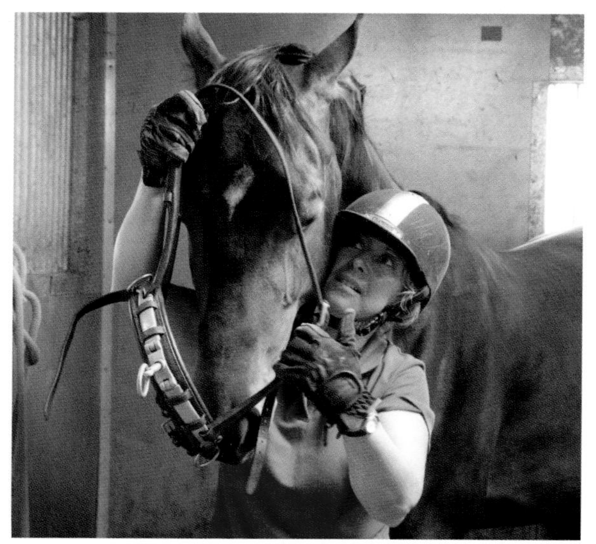

Above left In this photo, I am removing Mr Foley's headcollar in preparation for putting on his lunge cavesson. I prefer to take the headcollar off completely rather than fasten it around the neck, as I find that horses can pull back with it around their neck and start fighting. This is the advantage of teaching your young horse to stand still when you want him too. He has his eyes shut in this photo – don't worry – I am not poking him in the eye!

Above right A reassuring hand around the nose keeps Mr Foley's head steady.

Left To prepare for putting on a bridle at a future stage, practise putting the headcollar and lunge cavesson on over the ears.

Also teach him to move over in the stable from pressure with your hand against his side in the exact spot your leg would be when riding. This is good preparation for future work.

In the school

Generally speaking, if I have acquired a new young horse at an early stage of training, I stable him for a couple of days to acclimatize him to his new surroundings before turning him out. During this time, I find it a good idea to teach the horse to lead in hand, and to move over from pressure against his side, or from a tap with a whip, before attempting to lead him to the field. This should follow on from obedience training in the stable. If he has become used to being tied up, and learnt that pulling back is pointless, he should lead in hand quite happily and not try to break away from you. If he does get excited by his surroundings, or the weather, it should be simple to keep him under control with a couple of firm tugs on the rope, and a firm word or two. Your horse needs to learn to lead beside you and to keep out of 'your space'. This prevents you from getting trampled should he get a bit excited. Lead the young horse in a 'close lunge position' facing towards his shoulder, with the whip carried alongside his body. From here it is easy to send the horse forwards on to a circle rather than pushing into you.

Below left Leading confidently around the school.

Below right Learning to 'keep out of my space': leading Mr Foley beside me. Note that I am facing towards his shoulder in a 'close lungeing' position. Should be become over-excited, it is easy from here to let the line out so he can go forwards on to a circle rather than jumping all over me!

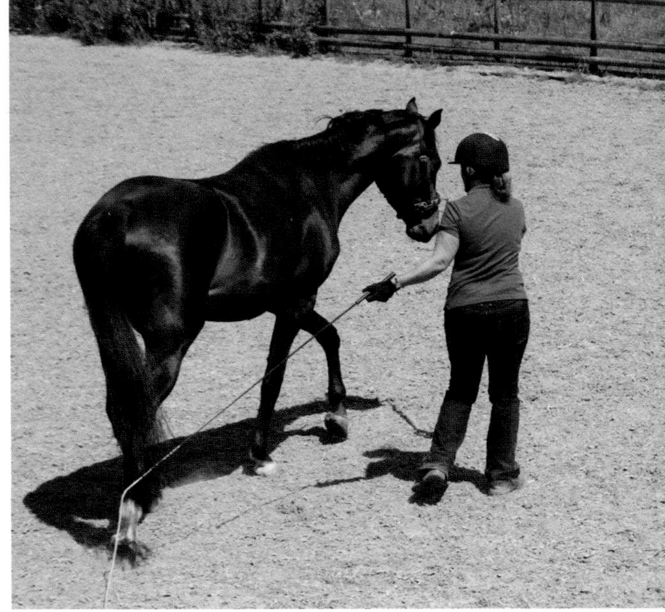

Make sure the surface on which you do your initial training is even and not full of holes. Young horses do like to put on a turn of speed, and the last thing you want is a pulled tendon, for example. Make sure that the surrounding fence is secure, and will not break if the horse runs into it, and that it is high enough to deter him from trying to jump it. Also make sure the gate is securely fastened and will not open should the horse barge into it. Good lighting is very important, whether indoors or out, as pools of bright light interspersed with dark shadow can make youngsters, in particular, quite spooky. Limit distractions by choosing a quiet time of day, especially in the early stages of training. The young horse tends to have a very short attention span of about a minute at a time, so you want to make the most of these brief flashes of co-operation, and not waste them by him neighing at the top of his voice to any horse close by who is looking for a bit of a chat.

Lungeing, leading in hand or long-reining with the tack on accustoms the young horse to wearing a saddle and bridle; gets him used to the feel of a girth around his belly, and a contact with the bit.

In the field

As just mentioned, make sure you have control of your horse in the stable and can lead him in control around the school *before* attempting to turn him out. If you are having obedience issues with your horse, it is not a good idea to let him charge to the field to let off steam: he will most probably break free

Below Lead your horse around the yard and through doorways calmly. This prevents him from injuring himself by getting caught on a doorpost, and you do not get squashed in the process.

Above Practising going through the school gateway before attempting it in the field.

while you are trying to lead him and could knock you over, or hurt himself. If your young horse is rather boisterous, a chain over the nose can help you to maintain control when leading him to the field. Of course, this should be rectified over time by training him to lead politely around the school.

Once he walks in hand sensibly around the school and stops when asked, lead him to the field in exactly the same way, using walk/halt transitions to keep his attention on you. It is preferable to turn him out on his own initially next to a field with other horses. This will provide visible company, whilst avoiding the skirmishes that can occur and cause injury should you turn him out directly into a field of horses with an established hierarchy. Once all the horses have introduced themselves over the fence and got over the initial excitement, your horse should fit into his place in the pecking order. If you *are* able to turn him out alone, make sure you have the field gate wide open before you lead him into the field. This will avoid the situation in which he could become excited and want to dive at the grass, and trample you as you try to open the gate! (It is also a good idea to practise going through gateways and opening and closing the gate in the school before attempting to turn the horse out into a field.) Also, make sure horses in the neighbouring fields are quiet before you turn him out. This avoids bucking and rearing etc. that the excitement of seeing his mates out already can cause. Alternatively, turn him out first, closely followed by a friend or two, so he is not left alone – yet another cause of wild behaviour! A toy or two can also be useful – a car tyre or rubber ball, for instance. Playing with something safe is far better than wrecking the fence!

Below left Under control and off to the field! Have your horse beside you so you can keep an eye on his behaviour. In this way, your horse learns to lead confidently. Having him trailing behind you teaches him to follow you as a leader, but not to be brave and to work as your partner.

Below right If your young horse is rather boisterous, a chain over the nose can help you to maintain control when leading him to the field. Of course, this should be rectified by training him to lead around the school.

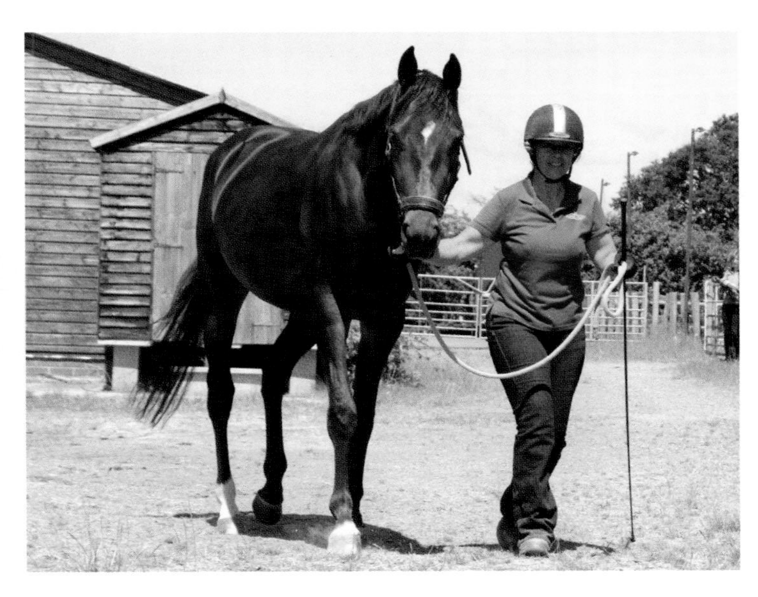

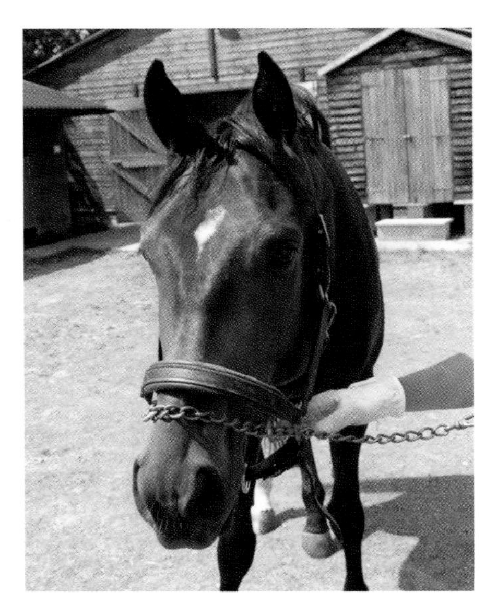

If your horse does make a bid for freedom when you are leading him to the field, it is better to let go rather than hanging on and breaking your arm. If possible, make sure that your horse is always in an enclosed space (use any walkways between fields, and close connecting gates) so if you do need to let go he cannot go far. This can prevent a power struggle between you and your horse – he will win every time and being dragged along the ground is no fun. It is far better to let your horse have some 'free time' to calm down, then retrieve him and start again with leading him calmly in hand. If he is naughty going to the field, 'mix and match' leading work both in the school and to the field and back.

When bringing him back in, remain calm, and expect him to come to you. Tit-bits should be avoided unless you want to be mugged every time he sees you. A kind word or two and a pat should be perfectly adequate to let him know you are pleased to see him. Lead him calmly through the gateway – again open it wide so he does not bang a hip on the post as he goes through. This can result in a horse who is afraid of gateways and anything resembling a gateway for quite a while. It is always best to avoid problems wherever possible, or you will spend ages correcting things that could so easily be avoided in the first place.

Below left Making a bid for freedom – rather than hanging on and breaking your arm, make sure your horse is always in an enclosed space so, if you do need to let go, he cannot go far. Letting go can prevent a power struggle between you and your horse – he will win every time.

Above It is far better to let your horse have some 'free time' to calm down, then retrieve him and start again with leading him calmly in hand. If he is naughty going to the field, 'mix and match' leading work both in the school and to the field and back.

Above left Catching a young horse in the field. Here I am attaching the lead rope calmly, and remaining focused on what I am doing.
Mr Foley, on the other hand, is contemplating whether to leg it, or stay with me.

Above right Safely in the yard and keen to go into the stable for lunch! It is important that your young horse waits for you to tell him what to do next rather than dragging you off.

It may help to leave his headcollar on for ease of catching – just clip the rope on quietly; otherwise you may find yourself faffing about trying to fit his headcollar. If you are not adept at putting it on quickly and quietly, you will end up with a horse who cannot be caught unless you leave a long length of rope hanging from his headcollar to grab hold of, or you spend five hours standing in the field with a carrot in the futile hope that he will stop eyeing you up from a distance and come to you willingly.

To begin with, just leave him out for an hour or so. Leaving him out all day to 'take the edge off him' will just result in a horse who reverts to the wild – forming a herd with his field mates, and forgetting all about you. Although each horse is different – some are perfectly trainable living out all the time – others forget who you are after half a day, it remains that case that the longer a horse is out, the harder it will be for you to be his 'herd leader'.

Building a relationship

There is nothing better than having an animal with whom you have total trust and a deep bond. In feature films or on TV this may appear to happen instantaneously – those of a certain age will remember *My Friend Flicka*, the horse who would come to the rescue, or *Skippy*, the kangaroo who could somehow convey messages such as 'The kids are trapped in the old mine'. In real life, however, trust and bonds take time and dedication to develop. Also, a good relationship can be ruined at the drop of a hat, with a misunderstood reaction between human and animal. Fear, mistrust, anger, frustration and haste are all enemies of a true partnership. I cannot recall a horse who was born 'bad', but know of many who have been spoilt by poor handling.

Unfortunately, some are affected by circumstances out of their owner's control, such as a road accident, or traumatic surgery for example, from which the horse cannot fully recover his former good character. 'Baggage' can affect a horse physically and mentally for his whole life. His memories may appear to fade, but often such a horse will have 'flashbacks' to a painful experience, or a situation he does still not understand. This can often be the case with 'rescued' horses. It may make you feel good to 'save' a horse, but this is not something to be taken on lightly. A lot of experience and patience are needed – and, often, very deep pockets! It is important to recognize that you may not be successful in turning your project into an Olympic contender, despite your best efforts.

That said, timing can be a very important factor in building trust. If a horse is in trouble, and you are there at the moment when you can really help him, he will latch on to you for life and be your best friend.

Avoiding misunderstandings

As mentioned above, when building a relationship with your horse, it is important to avoid misunderstandings – especially those based on rushing to judgement without checking the facts. You may find that, during this initial training, your horse may not respond as you expect – for example, he may appear to resent the bit, the noseband, or contact with side-reins – issues which may manifest themselves by him being fussy with his tongue, playing excessively with the bit, opening his mouth, throwing his head around, pulling on the bit and so on. In such cases, it makes sense to check his mouth for sore gums, or cheeks, and to see if he is teething (an issue often overlooked by owners of young horses). It may also be worthwhile consulting your vet to see whether wolf teeth are a contributory factor. A good way of assessing his acceptance of the bit is to put a bridle on him in the stable, hold the reins in your hands, and take up a gentle contact as you would for riding, and see how happily he accepts this. If he chews calmly at the bit, then this is a good sign that all is okay.

If he is ticklish when you are doing up a roller, or the saddle girth, just take your time. Spend short periods brushing and stroking him all over, then leave him in peace. It is far better to do this several times a day for just a few minutes than keep on and on, stressing him out.

Divide putting the roller on into small stages – fold it in half, lay it on his back, take it off. Lay it on his back, go around the other side to let it down, then fold it back up, and take it off. The next stage is to go back around to the nearside, and reach under his belly, take the end of the roller in your hand, and gently do it up loosely. Tighten it a hole at a time just so it will stay put, but on no account yank it tight, or you will have a problem for ever doing up your saddle girth. Take it off again. Repeat this lesson for a few days until he is perfectly calm and accepting of the roller. The same procedure should be followed with the saddle.

Young horses should not get back or neck problems unless they have had an accident. Correct training and good stable management should be sufficient to keep your horse in good health. Contact your vet if you have any worries.

Once you have reached the point at which your horse understands everything so far, and is confident with what he has learnt, he is ready to proceed with his groundwork training – in hand, on the lunge, and long-reining.

It takes time and patience to train a young horse. Once he is confident with what he has learnt, he is ready to proceed with his groundwork training.

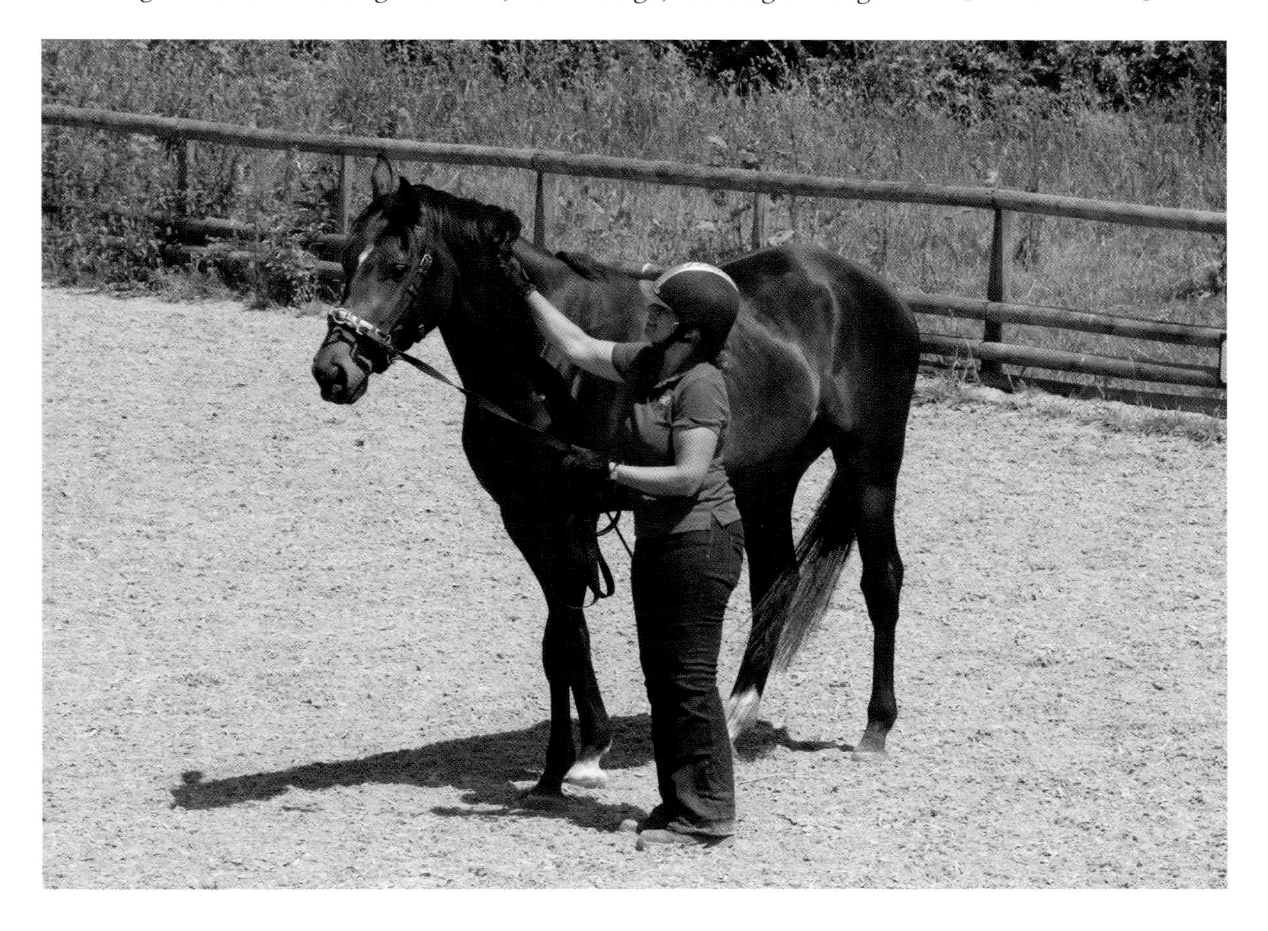

CHAPTER THREE

Groundwork Training for the Rider/Handler

You must be in the right frame of mind when handling horses. Giving friendly 'vibes' to your horse, and letting him know that you actually like him, will encourage him to work with you rather than against you.

GROUNDWORK FOR the rider/handler begins with the personal stuff – posture and mental attitude. Lungeing, long-reining and in-hand work are just as useful for teaching the rider as they are for educating the horse. If you are having problems riding your horse, you will usually find the key to the problem working from the ground. But before you come anywhere near a horse, there is an awful lot to learn about yourself, both physically, and mentally. Good posture is just as important when handling horses from the ground as it is in the saddle. You must also be in the right frame of mind. A stressed, tense person will have great difficulty handling their horse, so self-control is paramount. Giving friendly 'vibes' to your horse, and letting him know that you actually like him, will encourage him to work with you rather than against you.

In-hand work

With in-hand work, you are inevitably in close proximity to your horse, so it is very important that you are not afraid of him and have the presence of mind to reprimand him calmly if he gets a bit bargy to start with. In-hand work teaches you to maintain an upright posture at all times, with your core muscles strong, and to be balanced on both feet on the ground. Grounding yourself in this way helps you to be unaffected, mentally and physically, by any antics of the horse. You must also learn the importance of praise. The horse must be praised immediately by your voice, and a stroke on the neck once he responds as you want him to. Some people pat their horse very vigorously – this is confusing to the horse, as clouting him on the neck may be taken as a punishment. A gentle stroke is far kinder and much more effective.

Above left Here I am much too far to the rear of Mr Foley and risk being dragged along by him and, as you can see from his expression, his mind is elsewhere!

Above right A much better position to lead from. I have regained control by turning him towards me, and placing myself by his shoulder.

Your posture is just as important when leading your horse to the field as it is elsewhere. Just because the training session has finished, this does not mean that you let your guard down going into the field. Here, I am turning my body with Heinrich as we walk through the gateway, and concentrating on what we are doing. He is focused on me and walking quietly, not pulling or dragging me.

Whilst close proximity is integral to this work, it is important that you learn to keep the horse out of 'your space.' Imagining that you have a force-field of energy around you that the horse is not allowed to enter will keep him straight beside you, and prevent him from crashing into you. If he becomes pushy, focus on strengthening this force-field, and he will not crash into you. Try it – it really does work!

You will also learn to keep your shoulders back and down, and your arms relaxed. It is important not to hang on to the horse with the lead rein/lunge rein. A constant tight rein will make the horse tense, and he will want to pull away. To work a horse in hand, he must want to stay beside you on a relaxed contact.

Below Leading over a pole. Here I am close to Mr Foley to give him confidence, and my body language is directing him over the pole by having my leading hand encouraging him forwards, without hanging on to him, and my whip is carried alongside him to keep him straight, giving him no other option but to walk over it.

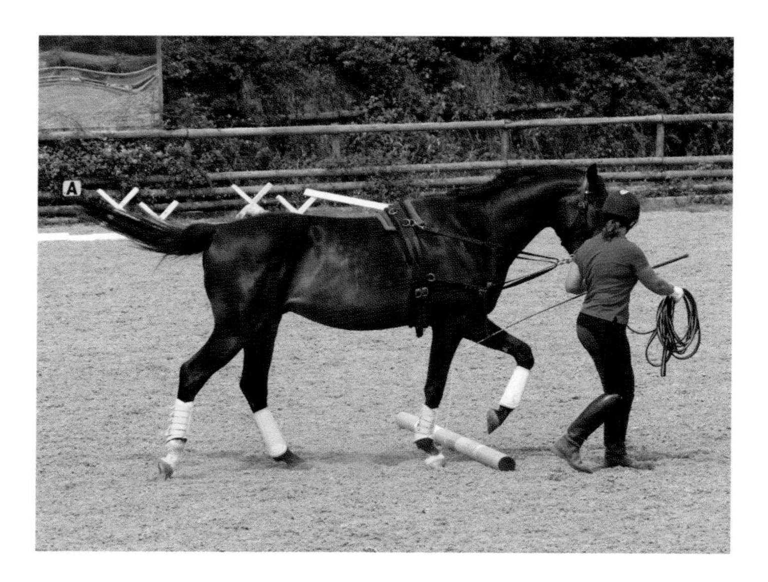

Above right Leading in a 'close up lungeing' position. Here I have my whip pointed towards Mr Foley's inside hind leg and am guiding him forwards with my rein hand on a light contact. My body is turned slightly towards him and I am watching his expression, and talking to him. Should he get excited and shoot forwards, I am in an ideal position to bring him around me on a small circle and lunge him.

Left Here I am in a vulnerable position, in front of Mr Foley. I look a bit worried, my shoulders are hunched and I am not standing tall. Mr Foley, however, is standing very quietly and waiting for me to sort out my rein and whip!

If, on the other hand, your horse does not want to stay anywhere near you, make sure that you are not exuding any of the negative feelings mentioned earlier (see page 33). If you are calm, in a good posture, and maintaining a light contact, small tugs on the rein, combined with bracing your back and firming your stance on the ground (in other words a half-halt) will bring his attention back to you if he becomes distracted by anything, or gets ahead of you.

For in-hand work it is important to place yourself by the horse's shoulder and to travel alongside him, facing either to the front or slightly to the rear, depending on what you are working on. Both leading him forwards and teaching him about rein contact require you to face slightly forwards, whilst keeping an eye on the back end to make sure he is straight. Asking him to step under behind in a halt, or teaching piaffe, for example, requires you to walk backwards, facing his back end, but you also need to keep an eye on the front end – i.e. his neck and head position, to make sure he is properly on the

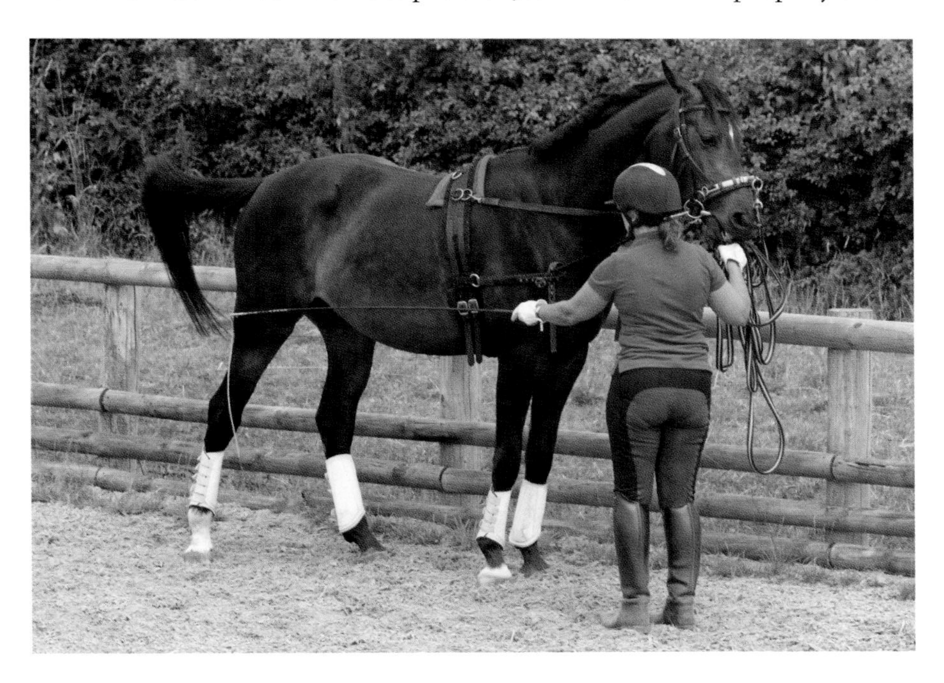

Here, I am getting Mr Foley used to the whip touching his hind leg – a preparation for teaching a horse to square up in halt, and later on, for introducing piaffe. I have him on a lunge rein should I need to let him have a trot around on the lunge to release any tension before he takes matters into his own hands! My stance is 'grounded' – I look secure on my feet, and calm. It is all too easy to get knocked over if a young horse gets a bit bargy, so always be ready to send the horse forwards on to a circle on the lunge to move him away from you so he is still working with you. It is important to repeat the in-hand work so you finish on a good note without letting him off the hook and thinking he is on a jolly!

Working in-hand with Heinrich in piaffe. My hips and shoulders are turned slightly towards him, and I am facing backwards so I can see his whole body. I am focused on what we are both doing, and even doing a bit of piaffe myself!

bit. You need to be aware of your shoulder and hip position, which should be turned towards the horse, but facing either slightly to the front or to the rear, depending on the exercise you are doing. You must be mentally 'on his side', calm and focused on what you are asking your horse to do.

Lungeing

Working on the lunge places you at a greater distance from the horse than in-hand work, but you still need to retain a high level of connectivity. Whilst rooted in mental focus, this is physically supported by the lunge rein attached to the cavesson/bridle, and by the lunge whip pointed towards the horse's inside hock, which, together with the horse's body, form a triangle with you at the apex. As mentioned earlier, you should be close enough to the horse to touch him with the end of the whip's lash. So, if you want to lunge him on a 20m circle, with its radius of 10m, and the length of your lunge rein and whip require you to be no more than 8m from the horse, you will have to walk a small (4m) circle yourself. (Don't think that you always have to remain rooted to the spot when lungeing – there are many times when this is not necessary, or even practical, as you will see in this book.)

When lungeing, you will learn how much the horse relies on your body language to tell him what to do. If you walk a small circle as he goes around

Here I am facing towards Heinrich when lungeing, with the rein and the whip forming a triangle with me at the apex. Note that my rein arm is maintaining a steady contact with the rein without pulling back.

you, he will walk. If you trot, he will trot; if you canter, he will canter. This body language works in conjunction with your rein contact and your whip aids (which are substitutes for your leg aids) in the same way as when riding. Your voice and mental aids are the same as when riding.

You will learn about keeping a contact to the bit or lunge cavesson, and maintaining correct flexion and bend. You will see whether your horse is struggling to bend to conform with the size of the circle he is on – are his haunches swinging in or out?

Lungeing also gives you the opportunity to observe your horse working. What you are feeling when you are riding him may not look how you imagined – it could be better, or worse! You can watch him stretching forwards and downwards, seeing if he really does take his nose forwards, and is not looking back at his knees (overbending). You can see if he is in a correct outline, his neck arching forwards to the contact with his head vertical to the ground, or just in front of the vertical, his back muscles working, and his hind legs taking weight under his body. Does he halt squarely or not? Are his transitions balanced or does he run into canter, for example. Using your body, rein and whip aids on the ground to correct these issues really does reap rewards when you are in the saddle. You will have a picture in your mind of how your horse looks, and have a feeling for the contact and, by evaluating the timing of your whip aids, an idea of timing your leg aids accordingly. Lungeing is a great rehearsal for schooling your horse from the saddle.

Time spent lungeing the horse can also give you a chance to calm down if you are feeling stressed before you ride. Similarly, if your horse is 'on one' and having a mad moment, lunge him to settle him before you ride, not by letting him charge around, but by making transitions, varying the size of circle and working all around the school. This is a good way to get him in the right frame of mind for ridden work, and is vastly different from the 'trotting rapidly around in small circles' referred to in the Introduction.

Here Norman is having a 'mad moment'. If this happens it is important to remain 'with' the horse mentally and physically. I am smiling, enjoying the moment with him, but ready to run forwards with him if needed. I am also aware that the lunge rein needs sorting out, but I am not panicking, or relaying this to Norman. It is important to realize that you will not stop a horse by pulling. This only makes matters worse and you will most likely end up flat on your face!

A few moments later, Norman is off having a spook. I am running alongside him, guiding him around on a large circle and waiting for him to settle. There is no point in trying to bring him around on a tight circle, as he would only become more tense.

A calm Norman free-schooling around me without a lunge rein. My body is facing towards him in 'lungeing position' and my whip is pointed towards his inside hind leg.

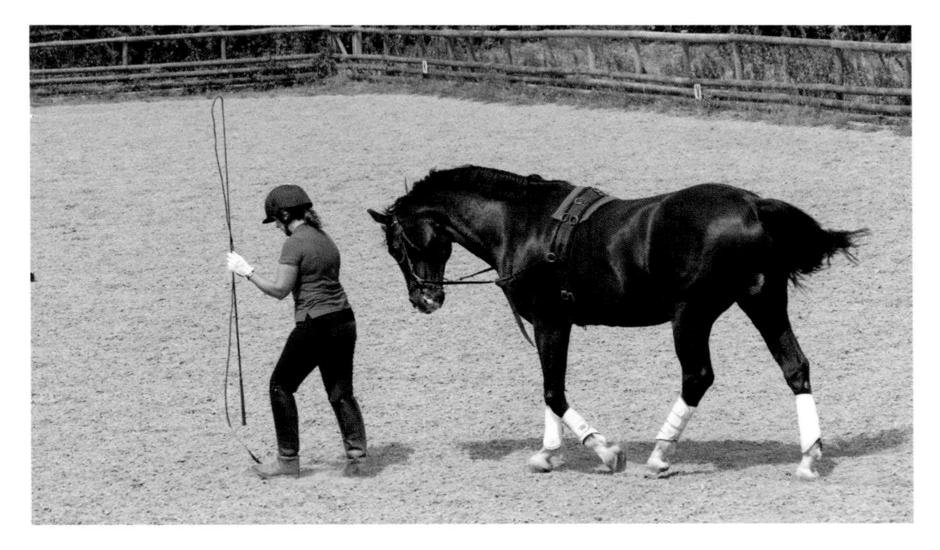

At the end of the free-schooling session, Norman follows me willingly towards the gate. His inside ear is angled towards me, showing he is focused on me. I am walking straight ahead without turning to look at him, and expecting him to come with me, so he does! After a few steps, I will stop and take the side-reins off so he can stretch before going back to the stable.

Long-reining

Long-reining helps you to develop a feeling for the rein contact. Maintaining an upright posture, with your arms in 'riding position', and balance on both feet – being grounded both physically and mentally – are all essential to learning about and establishing good contact.

If you pull, you will end up 'water-skiing' around the school behind the horse. If you are stronger with one arm than the other, the horse will spin around you. If you maintain an even contact with both reins, without pulling, the horse will walk forwards calmly, rounding his neck, and working into the contact. It is important to allow the horse to keep a light contact

Long-reining on a circle (double-lungeing) in good posture with the arms in riding position and balanced on both feet.

Left Here I am turning my body to face forwards with the horse, while still maintaining an even contact on both reins. It takes practice to handle a whip when working on long-reins, so it can help to start with a schooling whip first, and build up to carrying a piaffe or lunge whip.

with the bit with his mouth. You will learn how this feels, as any resistance or pulling, tension in your wrist and hands, is magnified by the length of the reins, so the horse will react adversely if you are doing any of these things. Doing movements such as shoulder-in, circles of all sizes, serpentines, figures-of-eight and so on all teach you where you should be in relation to the horse. It can help to imagine that you are on a train, with the horse being the front of the train, and yourself at the back of the train: you must both be travelling along the same railway tracks. With shoulder-in, if you turn your hips and walk in shoulder-in position yourself, your horse will also.

If you walk in leg-yield, crossing your legs with your body in right or left position, depending on which way you are going, your horse will walk in leg-yield. Replicating the aids for piaffe on the ground with frequent half-halts and taking small, raised steps with your own two feet will encourage your horse to take steps in piaffe himself. This may be hard to believe, but try long-reining a friend, and see how well they can feel what you are asking without you having to speak!

Above Shoulder-in on long-reins. Here you can see I have turned my hips and shoulders as though I was riding shoulder-in and am crossing my legs as I walk along the track behind Norman.

Long-reining is great for learning half-halts, (for both horse and rider) and how your body can block or allow forward movement. Your rein contact must be consistent – not pulling back, or dropping the contact. Your arms must work as a pair when blocking forward motion, but can soften individually to allow the horse to soften his jaw. It is important not to hold your horse up with the contact. If he is so unbalanced that he is leaning on the contact for support, suddenly dropping it will unbalance him even more, perhaps causing him to stumble. You have to feel when he is balanced – if you soften one rein and

Left Teaching the piaffe. Norman is balanced and working with loose reins. I am piaffing with him, with my feet doing what his hind feet are doing. I am reaching forwards with the whip to touch his inside hind leg to ask him to lift it off the ground at the next step, but keeping at a safe distance behind him in case he should he kick out.

his neck remains arched, and you can see the tips of his ears, he is balanced and on the bit. If you cannot see his neck, and he is pulling you, he is over-bent and on his forehand, so half-halts are needed to encourage him to take weight on his hind legs in order to raise his forehand.

Incorrect – pulling on the inside rein when long-reining behind the horse in an effort to control him will only make him crooked and he may well shoot off away from the direction he is facing, falling out through the shoulder.

Keeping Heinrich straight with an even contact. A horse inexperienced with long-reining can get alarmed if you suddenly disappear out of sight. It can help to walk slightly to one side of the horse so he can see you.

CHAPTER FOUR

In-hand Work

As THIS IS SUCH A VAST and important subject, I have divided this section into basic and more advanced work. Most problems handling, lungeing and riding horses can be sorted out with in-hand work.

Basic in-hand work

Basic in-hand work can be as simple as leading your horse to the field but, done correctly, things such as this can form an important basis both for building upon and for problem-solving. For example, loading issues can be sorted out with in-hand work. Instead of battling it out on the trailer ramp, you will be much better off perfecting in-hand work in the school with your horse.

Equipment

Developing a basic relationship with your horse, and establishing the basics of control and understanding, can be done in a halter or headcollar. The horse can be worked in hand from a bridle, lunge cavesson or a control halter. Side-reins are used to maintain the horse's outline when working in hand so that he develops the right muscles as he works. They help to regulate accuracy, balance and precision.

With stallions in particular, it is important to control the neck for the handler's safety. Stallions in the wild use their necks to fight with, and in domesticated situations boisterous stallions will head-butt the handler if they are allowed to do so.

In-hand work can be done in the field.

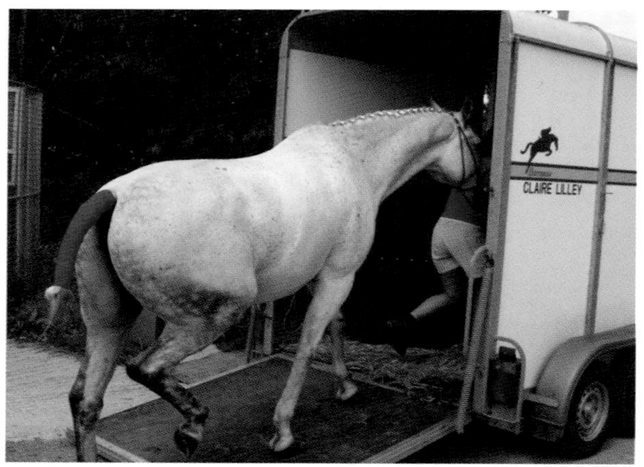

Left A horse who is well-behaved in hand is easy to load into a trailer or lorry.

For in-hand work, you will have your horse tacked up with a roller (or saddle if you are going to ride him afterwards), snaffle bridle, lunge cavesson, side-reins and a schooling or piaffe (driving) whip. The side-reins should be non-elastic – horses can learn to pull against elasticated ones, and plain leather or webbing ones help the horse to keep a steady contact with the bit. The whip should be long enough for you to be able to touch his hind legs when you are working with him by his shoulder. You can use either a lunge rein, lead rein or lead rope for in-hand work, but a lunge rein is useful if you want to intersperse in-hand work with lungeing during the training session. If your horse is strong-minded and has little respect for you, and you are likely to need to give firm half-halts, use a lunge cavesson rather than connecting the line to the bit. You can then give him a good tug on his nose if necessary, which you would not want to do if you had your rein connected to the bit. Only work your horse from the bit once he understands half-halts on the cavesson and responds to more subtle rein aids.

It takes many sessions to gradually build up concentration and relaxation, so several short spells of in-hand work, a couple of minutes at a time to start with, interspersed with a brief trot around the school on the lunge are useful for relieving any tension build-up in the horse, or in yourself.

In-hand work starts from a lunge cavesson with a young horse.

Below Using a Be-Nice halter for in-hand work is another option.

Lead from the shoulder so you can observe your horse's expression at all times.

Leading Norman as a warm-up before riding. Walking with your horse loosens you up as well as getting you both in the right frame of mind.

It depends on the horse whether you start with in-hand work or lungeing. If he is calm, then you can begin with in-hand work. If he is a bit lively, and likely to trample all over you, it would be wiser to lunge or free-school him (see page 99) him first and only begin in-hand work once he is settled.

For in-hand work, begin without the side-reins attached to the bit, but clipped on to the roller/saddle. Have them adjusted to the correct length before you start – so the horse will be in a correct, rounded outline with his poll the highest point, and his nose vertical, or just in front of the vertical, once you begin work with the side-reins attached. The side-reins should be attached to the roller in such a way that they are horizontal to the ground when the horse is 'on the bit'. They can be used once the horse is loosened up and relaxed enough to accept the contact, although if the horse is playing around as you are leading him, and there is a risk of him charging off or pushing you over, it would be safer to put them on before you start. If your horse is really difficult to lead out of his stable, then put the side-reins on in the box. A rude, bolshy horse can be very dangerous. Discipline is necessary, and most will settle to work quickly once they realize they are not leaving their stable for a play in the field, but are going to learn in the school.

Response to the aids

Teaching your horse to be responsive to the rein, whip and body aids is essential to successful groundwork, but just as important is focus and mental concentration, from both you and your horse.

Start the training session by leading your horse around the school, preferably without side-reins (but, as mentioned, fitted if necessary to help you keep the horse under control), making transitions between walk and halt. Facing forwards, hold the rein in the hand nearest the horse, with a light contact. Have the slack of the rein in your other hand, along with the whip, which should be carried parallel to the horse's side. Beginning with your leg nearest the horse, take a step forwards. As he sees this leg move, he should walk forwards with you. If he does not, put your leg back where it was and stand still again. Repeat a few times, until he walks forwards slowly with you. If he does not, tap him smartly with the whip, just enough to get a reaction, but not so much that he shoots forwards. Walk confidently forwards and expect him to come with you. Think, 'walk on' as you do. Look straight ahead. Avoid pulling him along, and stay by his shoulder. Do not get ahead of him or look him in the eye. If he walks too fast, use half-halts on the rein (see below) until he stops, making sure you release the contact in between each one, i.e. tug, release, tug, release. To halt, first take smaller steps, with a half-halt as you take each one, which will encourage the horse to take shorter steps in preparation for the halt transition, then stop moving. As you stop, your horse should stop. Make sure you are thinking 'stop' also. If he does not, give a firmer tug on the rein, and use your voice, saying 'stand' in a calm, commanding manner. There is no need to shout or to panic. If you do not prepare for the halt calmly, and stop suddenly, hanging on to the rein, your horse will do a 'handbrake turn' turn

Praise for tackling something new. As you see, Mr Foley can raise his neck as he needs to, but I still have control over his outline without him being restricted.

around you. If this happens, push him away with your hand against his neck so he is straight on the track and start again.

Half-halt

A half-halt is a co-ordinated action of your body and rein aids which balance the horse so he takes weight behind. Responding to your aids is as essential to groundwork as it is to riding. On the ground, a half-halt is done in the same way as you would from the saddle – brace your back, close your elbows to your sides, maintain a steady contact with the lunge rein/lead rope, and keep your weight down into your feet. On board, you would keep your weight into your stirrups and close your legs against the horse's sides. On the ground, brace your legs into the ground. Keep your abdominal muscles firm, as you would when riding. Once the horse stops when you do, soften your muscle tone and go forwards again, with the horse. In a nutshell, a half-halt is a 'stop, go' action.

Teaching your horse to halt squarely

Once your horse walks and halts beside you and understands half-halts, you can teach him to halt squarely. You can do this as an obedience exercise without side-reins, but to develop the horse's strength and balance, correctly fitted side-reins will keep him in a rounded outline, so he uses the right muscles. With the hind legs placed under the haunches, taking weight, the horse will engage his 'core muscles', i.e. his abdominal and back muscles. As a result of this engagement, he will arch his neck forwards into the contact with the bit with his poll the highest point and mouthing the bit quietly, with a relaxed jaw.

We will start on the left rein, as most horses are used to us doing things on their nearside (although you should do everything on both sides of the horse so he does not become one-sided). Bring the horse to a halt, on the track close to the school fence or wall, to keep him straight. Stand by his shoulder, facing to the rear, with the lunge rein in your left hand, nearest his head, and your schooling/piaffe whip in your right hand, holding it alongside his body, so you can touch each leg in turn with the tip of the lash. If he has 'left a hind leg behind', give it a little flick with the whip on the back of the cannon bone. He should respond by raising this leg, and placing his foot further forwards, under his haunches. If he does not respond, repeat the whip aid a few times until he moves his foot. He may not put it forwards enough, or may step backwards. In this case, quietly repeat until he places his foot in exactly the right place, under his haunches. If the other hind foot has 'fidgeted' out of position, you may need to repeat the process with that one. If you cannot reach across behind his near hind, and touch the rear of the off hind cannon bone, then reach in front of the near hind, touching the front of the other cannon bone. This works perfectly well. Just remember to do the same thing when you repeat this exercise on the other rein. Once both hind legs are parallel, under the haunches, praise your horse, and lead him forwards in walk.

He may not halt squarely in front. In which case, touch the forefoot that is too far forwards or back, so the horse lifts it up, and places it square to the other one, under the shoulder. In a square halt, all four legs should be vertical, and not slanting forwards or backwards.

When training the horse to halt squarely, it is important to end the session once he is standing quietly and squarely, or as squarely as he can manage. Going on for too long can cause the horse to become tense and fidgety, and he will not stand still, becoming anxious when you bring him to halt, instead of being relaxed. If your horse learns that standing still is a time when he can settle his mind, then he will halt easily for you whenever you ask him to, whether on the ground or ridden. Standing still is difficult for a horse. Being a flight animal, his natural reaction is to run away, so if he will halt with you this is a sign of great trust. Once he stands still, undo the side-reins, and walk him forwards, finishing the training session by allowing him to stretch.

Touching the hind leg to ask Mr Foley to pick it up. Now he is starting to work into a contact, I have more control over his topline development.

A square halt in a good outline for a young horse, with the nose slightly in front of the vertical.

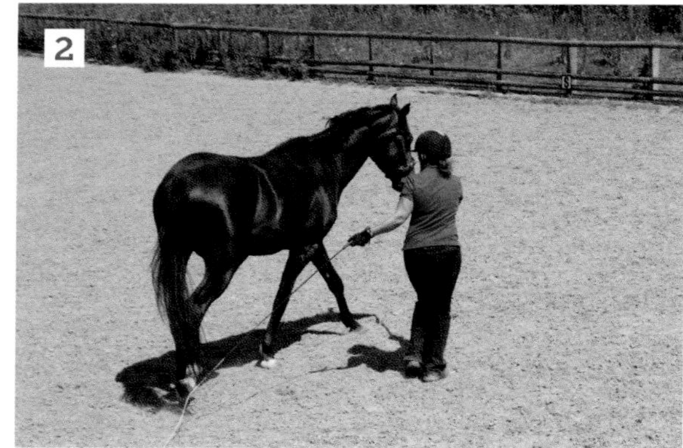

1. Starting a circle, about 10m in diameter, in hand with Mr Foley.

2. Carrying the whip close to his hind legs to make sure the hind feet follow the tracks of the forefeet.

3. Guiding his nose around the circle line. Note that my body is in 'close up lungeing' position, which prepares him for lungeing at a later stage.

4. Further around the circle he is turning his neck towards me a bit too much.

5. Here, I am using the front of my body to 'project energy' towards his middle to get him to move his body out in line with his nose in order to straighten him up.

6. Here he is straight again, with his whole body on the circle line.

Circles

Correct circles are a prerequisite for lateral movements. Lateral work should not be attempted until your horse can execute perfect circles on both reins, making sure he is supple in both directions, and understands how to work into the contact, accepting support from the outside rein and not relying on the inside rein for flexion. The function of the inside rein is to prevent the horse from looking to the outside, not to force him to flex to the inside of the circle – and it is a bigger error yet to try to pull him round with the inside rein. That said, it is important to use both reins, and not to be afraid of using the inside one as needed. If your horse is looking to the outside, the inside rein must be used to counteract this, and to keep the horse's head and neck in line with the body on the line of the circle.

The sequence of six photos on the opposite page shows how to progress with this work.

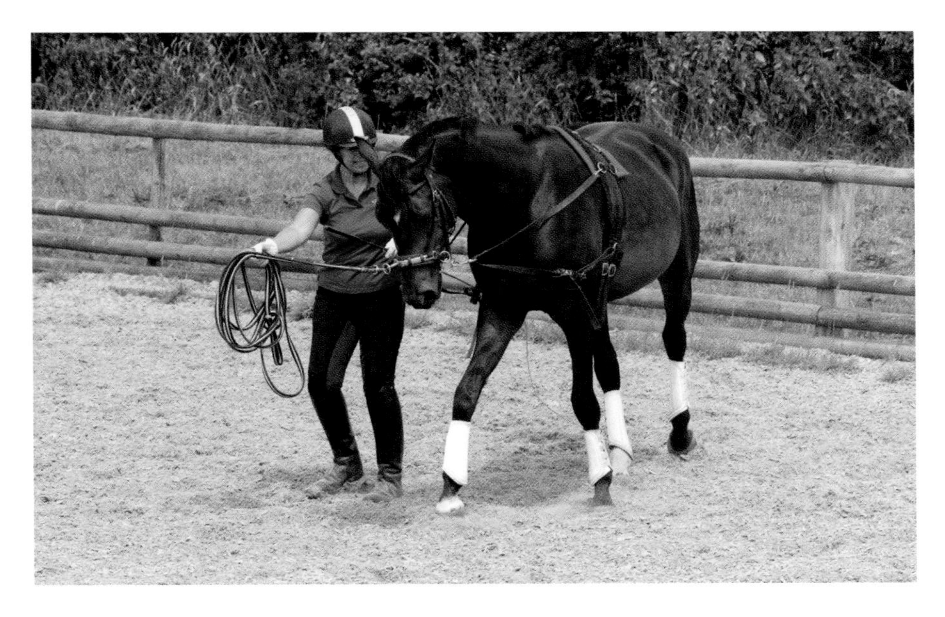

Mr Foley working in a type of side-rein called a Vienna rein or slide-rein, which has two anchor points on the roller, giving the horse the freedom to move his neck higher or lower, within reason, so his outline can vary without him getting out of control. Useful for a young horse, or a horse who needs confidence working into a contact. I am guiding him forwards on to a small circle with my lunge rein.

More advanced in-hand work

Rein-back

Once you have established the horse's ability to perform square halts, he can be taught the rein-back primarily as an obedience exercise (as distinct from a muscle-building one). No side-reins are used at this stage as the emphasis on muscle-building comes at a later stage. Bring him into halt parallel to the school fence or wall, which will help to keep him straight as he steps backwards. To ask him to step backwards, stand in front of your horse and, with the hand that is holding the rein, press with the tips of your fingers in the middle of his chest, saying 'back' as you do so. Give a few prods with your hand, and he should take a step or two backwards. Praise him. *On no account pull him back with the rein*, as he will learn to resist, and may rear up, or barge into you as a reaction. Carry your whip across the front of his chest as an extra aid, which effectively blocks forward movement, but 'opens the door' for him to go backwards. If he swings his haunches in, becoming crooked, place your whip parallel to his side to keep him straight. Ask for just one or two steps at first, building up to one horse's length before halting again. Re-establish the halt, so he is square, then walk him forwards again. This makes sure he walks forwards calmly, and does not shoot forwards after reining-back.

1. Mr Foley's attention is on me before attempting rein-back.

2. Look how much the joints of the off hind bend as he steps back on to it.

3. A good example of 'lowering the hindquarters'.

4. Stepping back with a rounded topline. See how muscles on the upper half of the neck are working as he rounds his back, and note how the abdominal muscles are tightening to support the body from underneath.

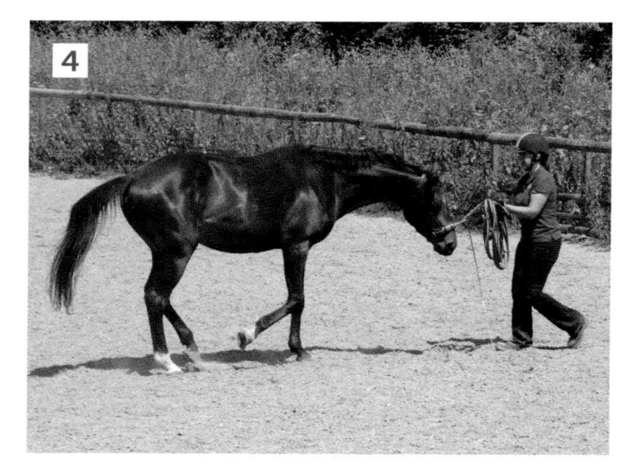

With a more experienced horse, side-reins can be used to maintain a correct, rounded outline so he develops strength through his back and learns to take more weight behind.

1. Here, you can see that Heinrich is hollowing his back at the beginning of the rein-back. He is taking weight on the near hind, off fore diagonal as the off hind and near fore move backwards in a diagonal pair.

2. As I ask him to step back, he tucks his loins, and you can see how his hind leg muscles are working as he takes weight behind. His neck relaxes and arches forwards to the bit. Here the weight is on the off hind and near fore as the left hind and right fore moving backwards in a diagonal pair.

3. The next step backwards – see how much Heinrich has raised his back.

4. Here his neck has raised from the withers to complete the picture of a correct collected outline with a rounded topline.

Turns around the forehand

Teaching your horse to move away from pressure helps to establish a correct response to the leg aids. Bring your horse to halt in the middle of the school, so you have room to turn him around you. Starting on the left rein, standing by his head, either directly in front of him or slightly to the left, face the rear,

Lateral work starts on the ground. Crossing the legs is a good suppling exercise for the horse's back. Here the turn around the forehand is done in the field.

with your lunge rein in your left hand, and your whip in your right, with it parallel to his side. Touch the side of his left hind, on the thigh. As you do so, flex his head to the left with the lunge rein.

Doing turns around the forehand without side-reins is a useful obedience exercise, with the horse yielding to pressure from the lunge rein and either the whip, or your hand against his side, but you will get a lot of neck bend. To make a turn around the forehand with lateral flexion at the poll to the left, and to teach the horse to work into the outside rein by yielding to pressure at the girth, he needs to work into a rein contact with the bit, whether this is with both side-reins, just the outside one, or with your hands holding the bridle reins. See the sequence of five photos opposite.

So, we will do this turn around the forehand to the left, with both side-reins on. They should be the same length. As the horse flexes to the inside, and steps across under his body with his inside hind, he will take a contact with the outside rein for support. The contact with the inside rein will become lighter, even to the point at which the rein is loose. The side-reins should be short enough to prevent the horse from bending his neck too much to the inside – a guide is that his inside nostril should come no further to the left than the point of his inside shoulder.

Photo sequence opposite ➤

1. The beginnings of lateral steps on a circle – a large turn around the forehand. This teaches the horse to move away from the inside aids on a turn or circle, which is later essential to ridden work. Note that I have a short rein contact to keep Mr Foley's nose close to me. My whip is held alongside his body to encourage him to step away from it sideways.

2. His near hind leg steps across under his body. He has raised his head as he is not sure what I am asking him to do because this exercise is new to him, although his expression looks trusting.

3. Here he takes a huge step sideways, and is giving me a bit more 'space' with his head, having moved away from me slightly into a better position. Too close, and you risk being head-butted or bitten!

4. Here he starts to relax as he gets the idea of stepping sideways around me, and looks much more relaxed.

5. A beautiful lateral step, showing how the near hip lowers as the near hind steps across. This work is so good for making the horse supple at any age.

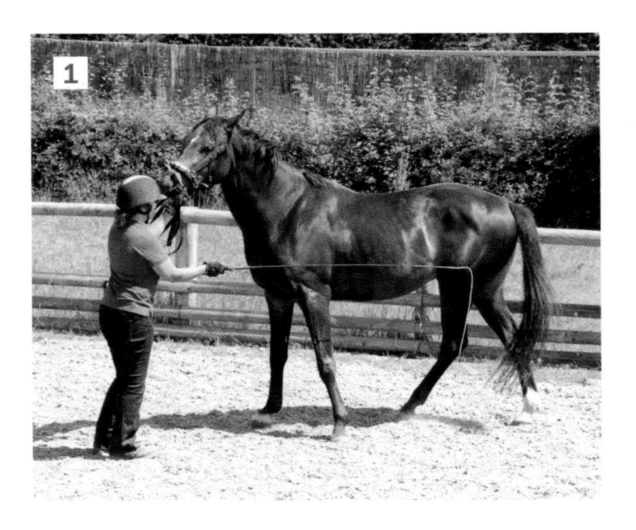
1

2

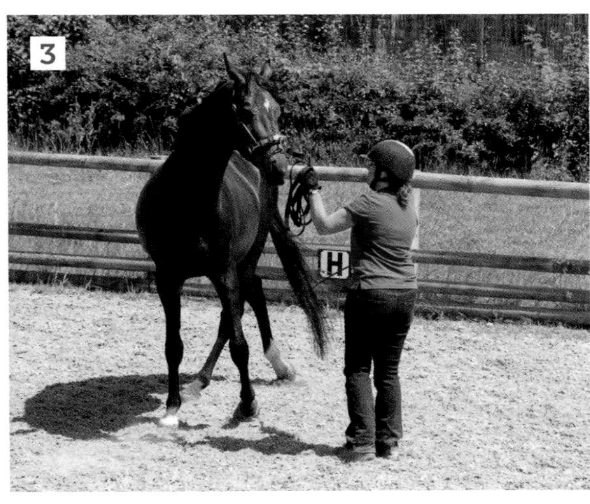
3
H

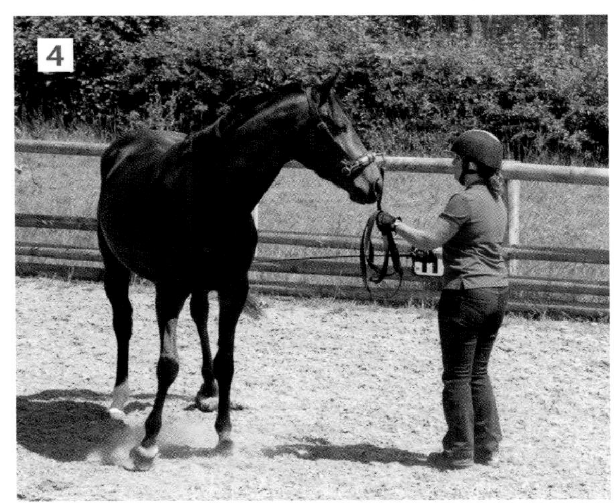
4

5
H

You can work him either from a lunge cavesson, or the inside bit ring.

Keeping flexion to the left, tap his inside hind, and say 'sideways' or 'over', whichever you prefer (but be consistent). As he takes a step sideways, stop and praise him. Ask for another step or two, then praise him again. Build up the turn around the forehand in this way until he can make a complete turn around you. His forelegs should also move, taking small steps to the side. The hind legs will take bigger steps as he moves around you.

Walk him forwards, halt him on the right rein, and repeat the turn to the right. It is worth noting that, like rein-back, turns around the forehand can indicate stiffness/one-sidedness. It is not uncommon, especially with fairly young horses, to find that they will turn much more readily in one direction than the other. If you find that this is the case, do not assume that your horse is being 'stupid' or 'obstinate' – treat it as feedback and note how the turns 'even up' as he becomes more supple.

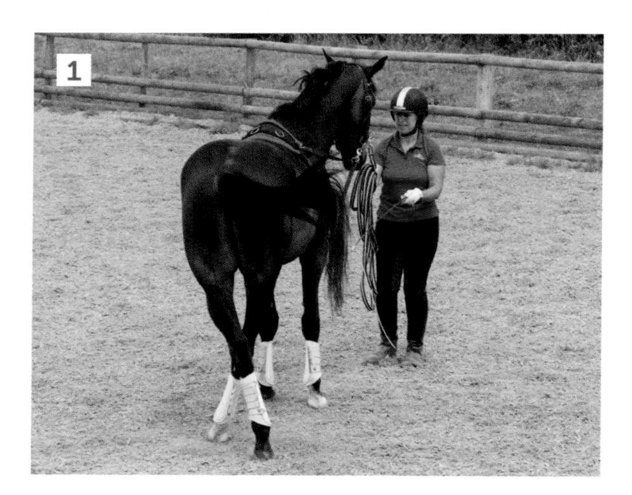

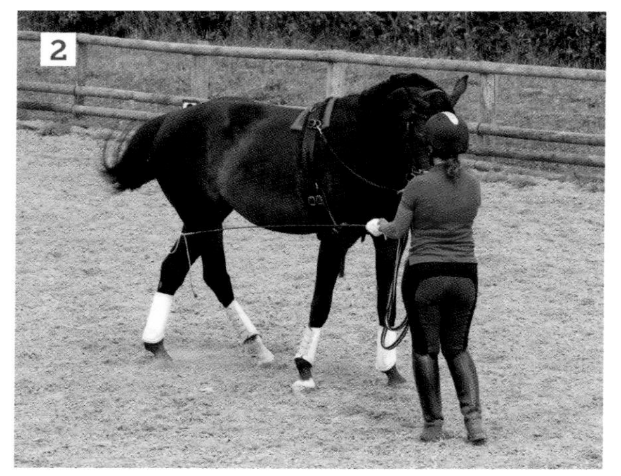

Shoulder-in

Shoulder-in teaches acceptance of the outside rein. The horse also learns to move away from pressure by the girth where the rider's inside leg would be, which produces bend, improving the horse's lateral suppleness. In shoulder-in, the horse steps forwards under his body, taking weight with the inside hind, which lowers the haunches, developing collection.

The side-reins should be the same length – the outside rein prevents too much neck bend, and the inside rein prevents the horse from looking to the outside and losing flexion at the poll. It is important that the poll is the highest point, to ensure a correct outline. If the front end is correct, the back end should function properly – with the hind legs taking weight, and the inside hind stepping forwards and under the horse' body. The whip should be used to tap the inside leg to encourage this. Half-halts keep the walk collected.

Keep the walk slow enough so that you can make sure each step is accurate. Keep your horse working on three tracks, with his inside hind leg and outside foreleg on the same track. His forelegs should cross, but not his hind legs. If he brings his forehand too far off the track, there is a risk that he will swing his haunches out, and lose the bend in his body. This then becomes a leg-yield on four tracks, with both fore and hind legs crossing, as opposed to a shoulder-in on three tracks, with body bend.

When a horse is in the correct three-track shoulder-in required in competition dressage, his body will be at a mean angle of around thirty degrees from the track. When the movement is first introduced under saddle, many trainers start off asking for a lesser angle, known as shoulder-fore, to introduce the horse to the basic idea of the movement. However, this is more difficult to do in hand, because the horse may want to straighten up rather

◄ Photo sequence opposite

1. Using either Vienna reins (see lungeing photo page 94), or plain side-reins, gives me much more control over Mr Foley's outline and bend than in the earlier stages of working without them. I can make sure he bends through his body and flexes laterally at the poll as he begins to step sideways around me in a large turn around the forehand. Because I can control the bend, he steps accurately across under his body with his off hind leg.

2. A step or two further on and he is clearly showing the lowering of the inside hip as he rounds his loins.

3. Here you can see how the outside rein supports his outside shoulder and prevents him bending his neck too much, giving more controlled steps behind. Compare this to the previous sequence of the turn around the forehand without side-reins, where we had too much neck bend.

than stepping just slightly sideways. Therefore it is easier to let him grasp shoulder-in first and get him used to moving away from pressure by the girth and from the position of the whip alongside his body. Once he can move laterally in shoulder-in, reduce the angle so he is then in shoulder-fore.

To maintain bend, press the horse's body with your hand, just by the girth. If he does not respond to hand pressure with a closed fist, give him a poke with your fingers! This simulates the action of a spur, and is a useful way to teach the horse about spurs before you ride in them. You could take 'spur training' a bit further and hold a spur in your hand and just touch the horse with it to accustom him to the action. Be subtle – just touch him firmly enough to get him to move away from pressure; you are not to frighten him – remember a horse can feel the smallest fly!

Many of the principles applied to teaching a young horse lateral work are also applicable in other situations.

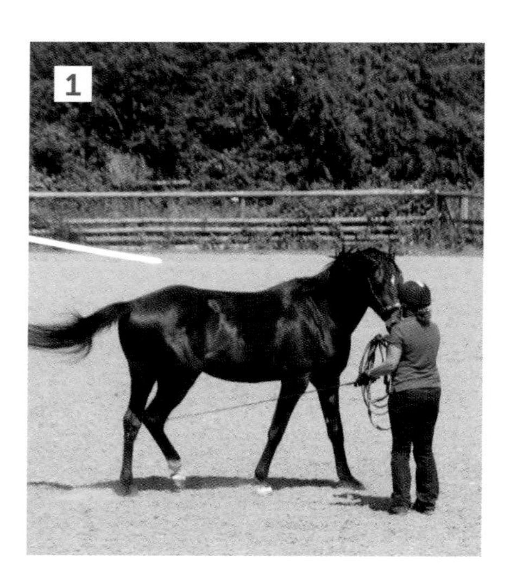

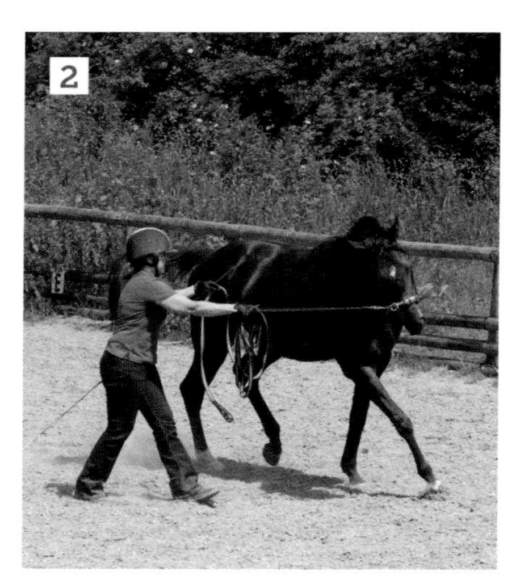

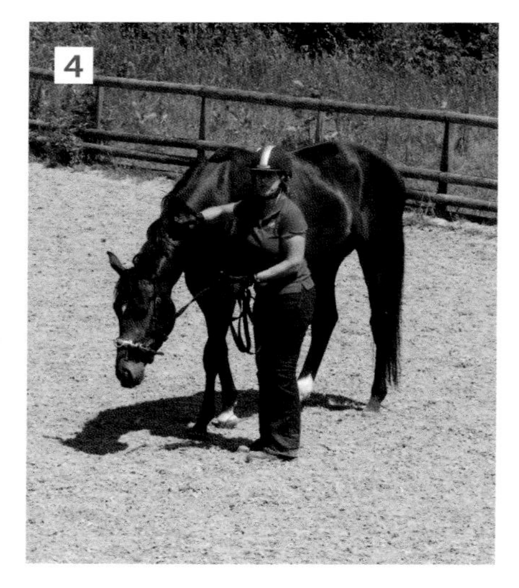

1. In the correct place for some sideways steps in hand – in front of Mr Foley's nose.

2. Here I have become 'left behind' and have little control over where he goes and at what speed! I am turning him around me to regain control.

3. The young horse must be allowed to stretch on a straight line when he needs to.

4. The end of the session. Mr Foley relaxed, and a bit tired, after working for about twenty minutes. A young horse has a short attention span and will tire quickly, so it is important to recognize when to stop. Always finish on a good note.

Piaffe

Once your horse can halt squarely, stand still and rein-back, he should have sufficient strength through his back and loins to take more weight behind, and learn to collect. Piaffe is invaluable in assisting the development of collection by taking weight behind on his haunches, and is preparatory work for passage.

Before starting to teach him to piaffe, loosen him up with some stretching work and walk-trot transitions on the lunge (see page 96). Then, make sure he is in a correct outline with side-reins attached, to ensure that he uses the right muscles. Make a few transitions from collected walk to halt in hand.

Halt him alongside the fence, which will help to keep him straight. Standing by his shoulder, in the same position as when teaching him to halt squarely, tap his inside hind leg – the one nearest to you – followed by a tap on his outside hind leg. What you want him to do is to lift and replace each hind foot in turn, until you have a 'one, two, one, two' rhythm going. Then, walk him slowly forwards, and continue to tap each hind leg in turn until he does one or two trot-like steps, in diagonal pairs. Do not expect him to do this 'on the spot' as this is placing too strong a demand on his body, and is also mentally quite challenging. Allow him to move forwards with each step to keep him calm and to produce active steps. You will have to be quite good at running backwards for this – and, as mentioned earlier, it's a time to take your spurs off! If he does not understand what you want, your horse may try to trot away, or to go backwards, which can happen if you go on for too

A precursor to teaching piaffe: a good square halt with a correct topline – the neck is raised from the withers and arched forwards to the bit.

long, so he becomes tense. So ask for only a couple of steps at a time. Halt him, and praise him as soon as he produces these.

When raising his hind feet, he should raise each to fetlock height, and appear to 'sit behind' as he lowers his haunches. As the back end lowers, so the front end will appear raised, and he will arch his neck forwards to the contact with the side-reins. His forefeet should ideally lift off the ground to mid-cannon height. He should quietly chew the bit. Use frequent half-halts to keep him beside you to prevent him from getting ahead of you, where you may lose control of him.

Once he gets the idea of moving forwards in piaffe-like steps, shorten the steps gradually, by using frequent half-halts, so that he travels only slightly forwards. An advanced dressage horse should be able to do 12–15 steps of piaffe travelling only a metre or so forwards in all, but this takes time to develop. In the early stages, as mentioned, just a couple of short steps

The diagonal movement of piaffe.
Upper photo Here, the near hind and off fore are raised off the ground. ***Lower photo*** Here, the off hind and near fore are raised.

will be enough both mentally and physically. Once this has been achieved, unfasten the side-reins, and allow your horse to stretch and relax, either walking him in hand, or lungeing him. If he has become a bit tense, he may need to trot or canter to release this tension, so that he finishes the session in a happy and calm state of mind. The same training can be repeated over several days – little and often is the key, rather than battling on for too long with both of you becoming hot and bothered!

In-hand exercises to try

EXERCISE 1

Starting at A on the left rein, halt, rein-back (purple line). Lead your horse on a three-loop serpentine, paying attention to turning accurately, and halt on the centre line each time. After reaching C, change the rein and repeat on the right rein (red line). Halt at A at the beginning and C at the end of each serpentine. To increase the difficulty of the exercise, from each of the halts, rein-back, and halt again. Proceed in walk. Alternatively, you could proceed in piaffe from either of the halts for a few steps, then continue in walk.

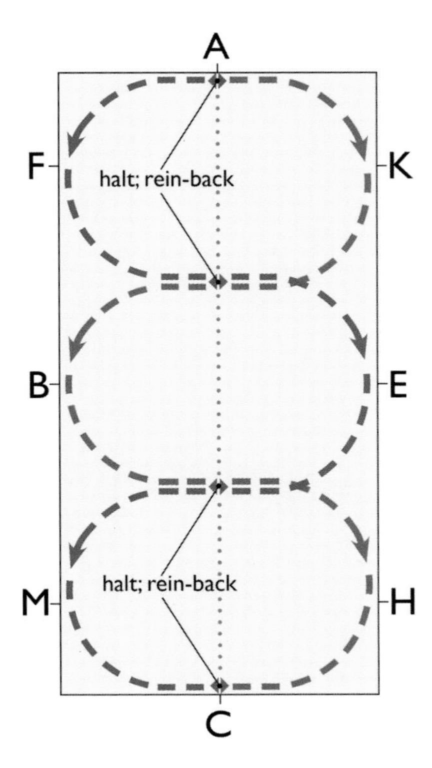

Exercise 1: Serpentine.

EXERCISE 2

Starting from A, lead your horse up the centre line (purple line). At X, lead him on to a 10m circle to the right, followed by one to the left (red lines), returning to the centre line. Before reaching the end of the centre line, ask him for a turn around the forehand (purple line). Repeat on the other rein.

EXERCISE 3

Starting on the left rein, lead your horse on to a 10m half-circle from just before K to the centre line (red line). This can be done either with no lateral steps, or in shoulder-in. Move him in shoulder-in along a diagonal line aiming to reach the track between B and M. On reaching the track, keep going in shoulder-in until M, then lead your horse on to a 10m half-circle and then on to a diagonal line reaching the track between E and K. Repeat on the other rein (purple line), starting just before H or F.

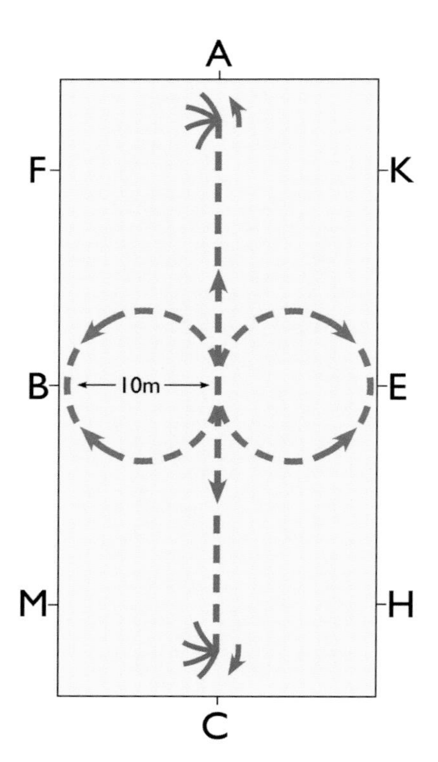

Exercise 2: 10m circles and turns around the forehand.

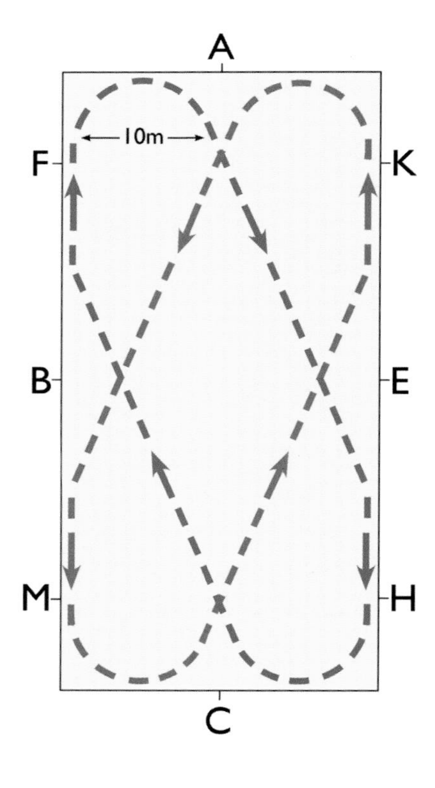

Exercise 3: Half-circles and shoulder-in.

Common in-hand problems and solutions

Barging, charging off, rearing, kicking out, etc. can be either an attitude problem, or a physical issue. It is very important to know the difference – for instance, is your horse rearing out of defiance, or is he in pain? Does he not understand? It is important first to give horses the benefit of the doubt, and look for a root cause, but if they *are* being naughty because they can get away with it, you must react accordingly.

Speeding up

If your horse walks too quickly he may lose the important four-time nature of the gait and, more pragmatically, you will not be able to keep up with him. He may shoot forwards once he realizes you have no control. If you pull on the rein, he may spin around you, and could knock you over. It is better to keep him under control to prevent this happening, by using several firm half-halts in quick succession until he is listening to you once more.

Lack of concentration

If your horse sticks his head up in the air and becomes distracted, for instance by horses galloping about in a neighbouring field, and is taking no notice of you, use several firm tugs on the rein to get his attention. They must be firm enough for him to react. As soon as he acknowledges your existence again, keep the rein quite still and light and praise him.

Contact issues

If your horse resents working with side-reins, first make sure you have them adjusted correctly. If they are too short, he will resist the contact. Alternatively, you could try using the bridle reins instead, with the outside rein passing over the withers. Hold these reins either in both hands when walking forwards so you can use them as you would when riding, or in your left hand by the shoulder if you are facing to the rear. You could also just use the outside side-rein as a support to keep the horse straight, and attach the lunge rein to the inside bit ring, so you act as the inside side-rein. You can then feel with your hand if the horse becomes tense in his mouth, and give soft half-halts to relax his mouth, encouraging him to mouth the bit.

Problems with halt

The horse may charge forwards and refuse to halt. If he does this, there are two options. You can let the rein out (this is the advantage of using a lunge rein for in-hand work) and lunge him for a few minutes until he relaxes, then resume the in-hand work. Alternatively, if you are quick enough to sense that he may run away, take preventative measures, by giving strong half-halts to get his attention, and to distract him from whatever it is that he feels the need to run away from.

Response to whip aids

The horse may kick out when you touch his hind legs with the whip. If he does this because he is angry, give a firm half-halt on the rein, and be stern with your voice – be authoritative, not angry. You could also give him a good smack on the offending leg with the whip. If he kicks again, smack him again. Once he stands still, praise him, and walk on. The smack must match exactly the strength of the kick from the horse. If it is too strong, you will just wind him up; too gentle, and he will take no notice of you. You will only need to apply this lesson once if you get it right. Next time you tap his leg, do it as gently as is possible to gain a response. Give him the chance to react calmly. Praise him. You have now fine-tuned your horse to respond to a light touch.

Remedial work

If any of the above problems cannot be resolved in between two and ten attempts, which can be spread over a few sessions, take into consideration that your horse may have a physical problem, or mental issues that are preventing him from responding to your aids as he should. For instance, a horse with back problems may have difficulty standing squarely. It is important to assess your horse properly as he halts. Is he having a bad day, and is 'not in the mood', or is there another factor? Teeth, back or foot problems are the most likely; although do make sure your in-hand work technique is not contributing to your horse's behaviour. He may just not understand what you are asking of him.

If the horse is weak in the back (and, indeed, even if he is not), the back muscles can be strengthened by walking very slowly and precisely, both with and without side-reins, so that the horse works with a relaxed neck, and in a correct rounded outline. Each step should be done in a very controlled manner. Walking over single poles on the ground is also useful. Rein-back, step by step, is also a good exercises for the back muscles, and helps the horse to 'tuck in his loins' which stretches the lumbar muscles. Rein-back can also be an indicator of existing problems – if the horse is crooked, or weaker on one hind leg than the other, he will not be able to rein-back in a straight line. Crookedness can also be a sign of weakness, lameness or stiffness through the back. Side-reins can help to keep the horse straight. Halt each time the horse steps to one side. Lead him between two parallel poles on the ground to help keep him straight, also halting between them.

CHAPTER **FIVE**

Lungeing

LUNGEING YOUR HORSE is not all about going round and around on small circles. It can incorporate straight line work, different sizes of circle, corners, and half-circles – in fact many of the movements in the school that you would ride can useful when lungeing. To use lungeing as a valuable gymnastic workout, aim to use the whole school during a session. A useful guide is to cover the whole area in hoofprints! Lungeing and in-hand work complement each other. If you have been successful in your in-hand work, you should now be ready to proceed with work on the lunge. Once your horse works well on the lunge, it can be interspersed with in-hand work to relax and also to motivate your horse – whichever he needs to do at the time.

Lungeing is not all about going round and around on small circles – use the whole school!

When you lunge, aim to position yourself so you are facing the roller/saddle, with your line and whip forming two sides of a triangle, and your horse the third side. You should be close enough to touch your horse with the lunge whip on his hind leg and also be close enough so that he is aware of your area of influence which is contained within the triangle. Your horse will know if your whip is 'out of range' – if you are too far away from him you run the risk of him losing his concentration on you and you will then have little control over him, especially if you allow your whip to trail behind him, smacking it on the ground or cracking it instead of touching the horse.

Keep the lunge rein coiled in the hand nearest his head, so it is easy to feed it out or shorten it as needed. It takes practice to handle a lunge rein with ease, using both hands to adjust the length while holding the whip. My old German instructor would lunge two horses at once and smoke a cigarette at the same time, although I am not recommending that you give this a try!

If your horse is well enough trained to react to the movement of your lunge whip rather than needing to be touched frequently, then you can remain in one spot, lungeing him at a greater distance, pivoting on your feet to keep your chest parallel to his body. However, as mentioned earlier, with a less well-trained horse, it is advisable to remain close enough to him to be able to touch him with the whip if necessary. Furthermore, you do not need to stay in one place all the time – move around the school to make different patterns, keeping control of the line and the whip at all times. Also, maintain an air of calm control so your horse trusts you.

Correct lungeing position – with me at the apex of a triangle between the lunge rein, the horse and the lunge whip.

Right Lungeing Norman on a straight line – down the long side in medium trot and *(Below)* bringing him back on to a circle again.

Stretching work

Lungeing your horse is a great way to improve his suppleness and relaxation. It is important that stretching work comes before working into the contact, to ensure his muscles are loosened and he is mentally calm. When stretching, your horse should extend his nose to the ground, as though looking for grass. All horses are able to graze, so all horses are capable of fully stretching their necks forwards and downwards.

Using a Chambon

As mentioned your horse should be able to stretch down to the ground, but he may not be able to if he is recently acquired and has had poor training in the past. If he is incorrectly muscled, often evidenced by a thick muscle under the neck, and a dip in front of the withers, he will not be able to stretch fully of his own volition, and he will need to build the right muscles, which takes time – anything from one to six months depending on how tight and pronounced these 'wrong muscles' are and how mentally scarred he is. Some horse will stretch when presented with a pole on the ground but, in many cases, a Chambon can be invaluable. It works on poll and bit pressure. If the horse raises his head and neck and hollows his back, he will feel slight pressure on his poll and the bit. As soon as he lowers his head, the Chambon loosens. The Chambon should be fitted so it is just taut when the horse's ears are in line with his withers, making it difficult to use the muscles under his neck, but easy for him to stretch forwards and downwards. As the horse stretches, he engages his abdominal muscles, which in turn brings the hind legs forwards under the body. It is best to loosen your horse on the lunge before attaching the Chambon.

The headpiece of the Chambon can be fitted to the bridle beforehand, with the connecting strap attached to the girth and fastened around the horse's neck when not in use at the start and end of the session. Pass the throatlash through the Chambon rings for loosening up and cooling off so

Loosening up in trot without the Chambon attached, with the horse's neck and nose stretched forwards.

they do not flap around. As the Chambon works on poll pressure, it is best not to have too much clutter on the horse's head, so lungeing from a bit connector attached to the noseband is a better option than a lunge cavesson in this instance.

When you are ready to use the Chambon, pass the attachment cord through the headpiece rings on both sides of the bridle and attach it to each side of the bit.

Once the horse feels the contact with the Chambon he will lower his neck. He may only do this in walk for a few steps at first, but eventually he

Thread the throatlash through the Chambon rings to secure them when not using the Chambon, when loosening up, or at the end of the session.

The attachment cord can be fastened around the neck when not in use.

Another view of loosening up before attaching the Chambon. You can see the attachment cord is fastened around Mr Foley's neck, and I have my lunge rein attached to the bit connector attached to the noseband. As the Chambon works on poll pressure, it is best not to have too much clutter on the horse's head, so I have not used a lunge cavesson over the bridle in this instance.

Left When you are ready, pass the attachment cord of the Chambon through the headpiece rings on both sides of the bridle ... ***Below*** ... and attach it to each side of the bit.

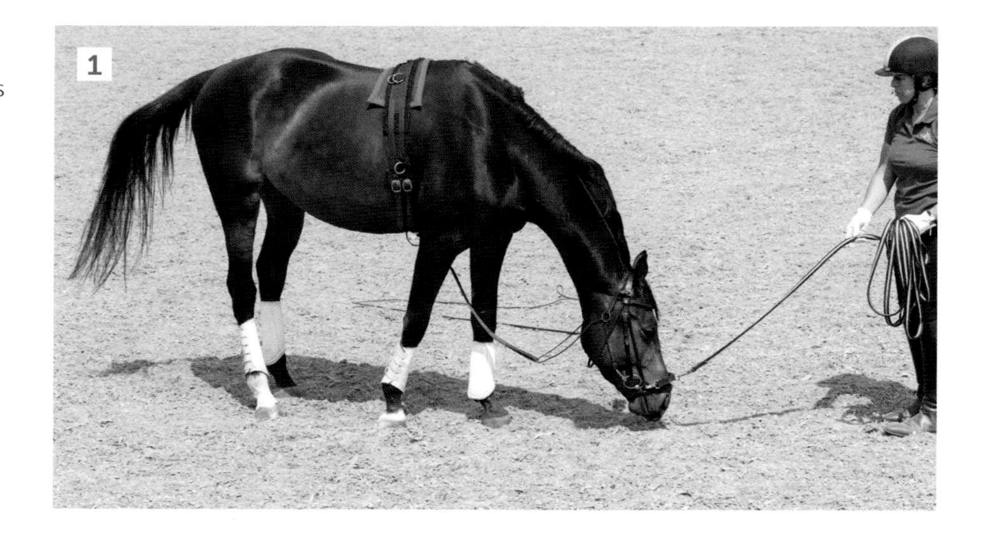

1. Mr Foley demonstrating how the Chambon loosens once the horse lowers his neck.

2. Stretching forwards and downwards with the Chambon.

Sequence continues opposite.

will be able to stretch in trot and canter once his muscles develop in the right way, and he gets strong back and abdominal muscles.

Once your horse has learnt to stretch down consistently, and his muscles are developed in the right way, you will no longer need the Chambon. Your horse will muscle up over his back and under his belly, as well as over the topline of his neck. His haunches will muscle up and he will work with his hind legs under his body, taking weight behind. As the neck lowers, the hind legs have to step under – otherwise your horse would fall on his nose. Because the horse cannot lean on the contact in the Chambon but is 'shown the way to the ground' he brings himself into balance as he tucks in his loins and engages his back muscles.

3. A lovely full stretch down with the Chambon in trot. The poll joint is totally relaxed so the nose reaches the ground.

4. In canter, you can see how the abdominal muscles are engaged and the loins tuck as Mr Foley steps forwards with his inside hind leg in this canter stride. The Chambon encourages him to work through his topline and prevents him from hollowing.

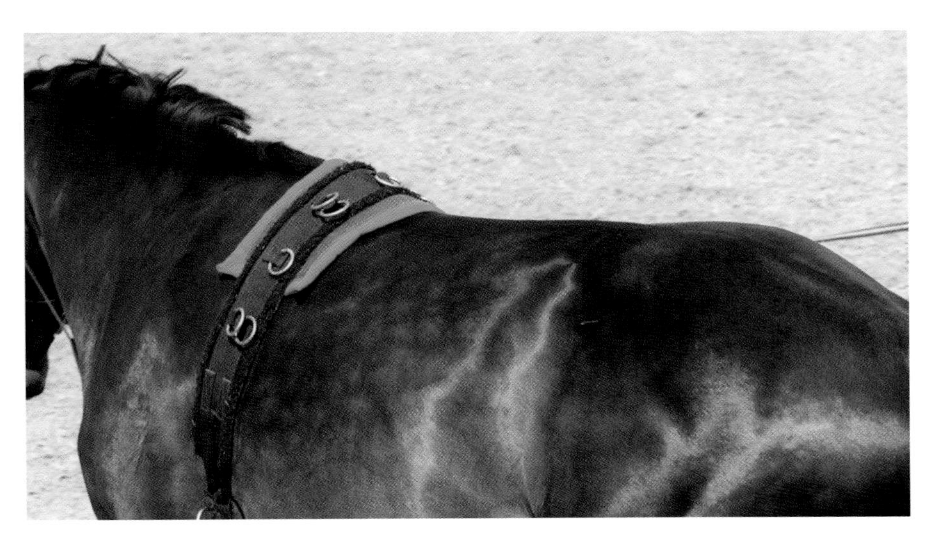

A strong back is developed through stretching work.

Establishing a correct outline with side-reins

Once your horse can stretch forwards and downwards, he will be strong enough through his back to work into the rein contact, 'on the bit'. Working in a correctly rounded outline develops the topline that many riders strive to achieve with gadgets, special feed additives, and so on, but there is no 'quick fix', only muscle development.

The purpose of side-reins is to *guide* the horse into a rounded outline – not to fix him into it. The horse should find the connection to the reins himself by working through his back. The side-reins should be attached so they are parallel with the ground when your horse's poll is the highest point, with his neck arched forwards from the withers and his nose either on, or just in front of, the vertical. The side-reins should be long enough to give the horse the opportunity to reach forwards into the contact at the beginning of a session. Once he takes the contact and chews quietly on the bit, the side-reins can be shortened a couple of holes to 'take up the slack'. As the horse rounds through his back, he will arch his neck a bit more, becoming rounder through his whole outline.

If your horse has never worked in side-reins, it is a good idea to start with just the outside rein attached. Have the lunge rein attached to the inside bit ring, as the inside rein. It is up to you to keep the inside rein contact to keep the bit straight in your horse's mouth and to ensure that he works into the outside rein contact. You will feel this quite clearly. If you loosen the lunge

Below left Attaching side-reins. They should be long enough for the horse to work with a rounded topline with the poll the highest point, and the nose vertical, or just in front of the vertical.

Below right Side-reins guide the horse into a rounded outline – they should not fix him into it. The horse should find the connection to the reins himself by working through his back. They should be long at the beginning of a session.

Shortening the side-reins to take up the slack after a few minutes.

Start with just the outside side-rein attached with the lunge rein to the inside bit ring.

rein, your horse will turn his head to the outside. If you take up the contact with the lunge rein, his head will be straight. It is important that you keep his head straight at all times.

It is a good idea to walk your horse around the school to get him used to equipment that is new to him. This the opportunity to assess whether what you are using is suitable for your horse at this moment. Throughout your horse's training you will constantly need to assess what is best for him.

Lungeing with just the outside side-rein attached is useful if your horse is not familiar with side-reins. This helps him to relax and accept the outside rein contact before you attach the inside rein.

It is a good idea to walk your horse around the school to get him used to equipment that is new to him.

Once your horse accepts the outside rein contact happily in walk and trot, you can attach the inside side-rein. Have both side-reins the same length. Shortening the inside rein can block forward movement in the same way as pulling on the inside rein when you ride, and can also result in the horse leaning on it and avoiding the outside rein contact, so I prefer to have side-reins the same length.

If your horse turns his head to the outside to avoid the outside rein contact, or has difficulty in flexing to the inside, you can use the lunge rein as the inside rein by passing it through the inside bit ring and attaching it to the girth. It is then down to your 'feel' for the contact to encourage correct flexion to the inside, so your horse's ears are straight on the circle line.

Using the lunge rein as the inside rein. This is useful to introduce the horse to the inside rein contact as you can soften the contact as required to help him to relax to the contact. Here, Norman is working beautifully, showing his well-developed topline.

Norman working in canter in side-reins. I have my lunge rein attached to the inside bit ring and the noseband so the contact acts on his nose primarily.

If your horse has contact issues when ridden – for example, he throws his head up when you take up a contact, or ducks behind the contact and overbends, he may well react in the same way with plain side-reins. Side-reins with elastic or rubber inserts are an option but, as mentioned earlier, horses can learn to pull against these and I prefer to use Vienna or slide-reins (see photo overleaf). These have two anchor points to the roller, and allow the horse the freedom to move his neck up or down to where he is comfortable. If your horse is tight through the back, or lacking in strength, expecting him to work with an 'advanced' outline placed from the start is unrealistic – he needs to work gradually towards this in his own time.

A useful alternative to straight side-reins – Vienna reins or slide-reins with two anchor points to the roller.

Right and below This type of side-rein allows the horse the freedom to move his neck up and down, guiding him into a correct outline, and acceptance of the contact. A useful alternative to elasticated reins which some horses learn to pull against.

Praise for Norman after working so well!

Free-schooling

For too many people, 'loose-schooling' means turning a horse loose in the school, shouting at him and chasing him around. Rather than this, you should think of free-schooling as lungeing without a lunge rein.

If your running abilities are limited, or your horse is too lively for you to handle, free-schooling is a good option. However, an indoor school is best, or a school with a fence high enough that your horse will not jump out if he is that way inclined. If you free-school without side-reins, you do run the risk of this, so for safety's sake side-reins are useful. There are two options here. With a lively horse, put the side-reins on before entering the school, and let him just get on with it. Once he has calmed down, go into the school and move near to him with your whip in 'lunge position' pointing towards his inside hind leg, and your other hand holding an 'imaginary' lunge rein. Connect mentally with him as though you had him on the lunge rein. He will settle (eventually) and you will be able to bring him to halt with your body language and voice.

If he does not come to you, or at least stand still so you can retrieve him, turn your back and walk purposefully to the gate, ignoring him. In no time, he will be following you. Once he stops with you, praise him and get to work, attaching the lunge rein and lungeing him as normal.

Free-schooling with Norman. My body position and whip are used exactly the same as when lungeing.

The other option is to free-school your horse at the end of a lunge session. It is a good way to practise your body language to see if you can work him in the same way without a lunge rein.

If you stand still, your horse should halt. If you take small steps, he should walk with you. If you 'trot' with your feet, he should trot, and if you take bigger steps, or 'canter' on your own two feet, so should your horse. If you stand still, he should halt with you. This game is great fun and it can be very gratifying to see that all your hard work reaps rewards and you end up with a happy horse who is totally in tune with your aids. This is a real bonus for ridden work also!

A lovely square halt. Note how my body language mirrors his and our halts are synchronized.

Here I am directing Norman towards the ground pole.

Directing him forwards in trot on a straight line.

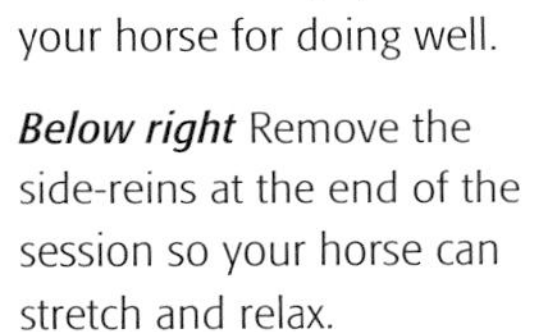

Below left Always praise your horse for doing well.

Below right Remove the side-reins at the end of the session so your horse can stretch and relax.

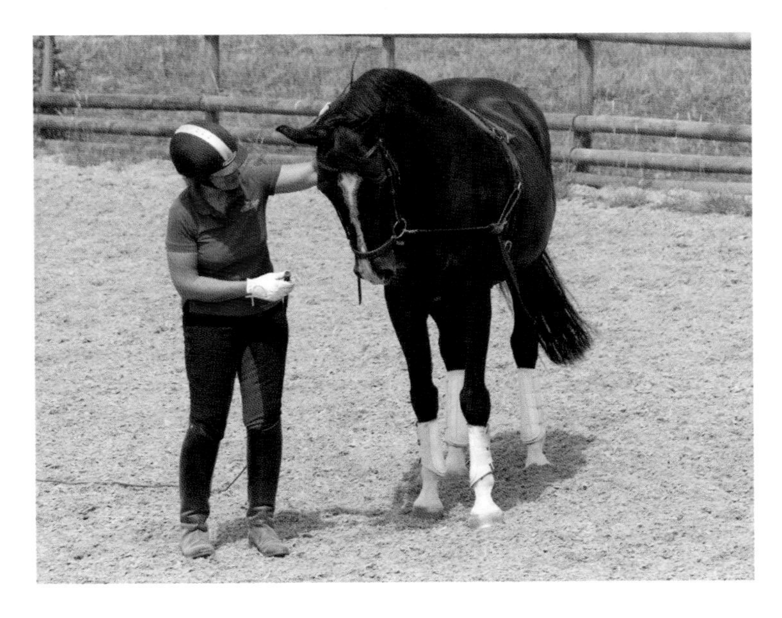

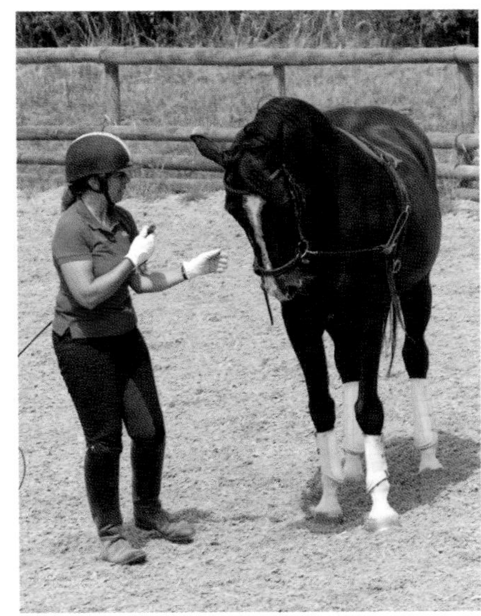

Lungeing exercises to try

These exercises can be done as stretching work either with or without a Chambon, or working into a rounded outline with side-reins.

EXERCISE 1

Lunge on a 15m circle (in walk, trot or canter) at the A end of the school twice around (blue line). Walk up the centre line yourself, with the horse travelling on a straight line parallel with the long side (red line). Make a second circle around X, the middle point of the school (purple line). Walk further up the centre line, with the horse travelling straight, as before (red line), and make a third circle at the C end of the school (blue line). Work your way back up the school with three more circles, finishing at A. Repeat on the other rein.

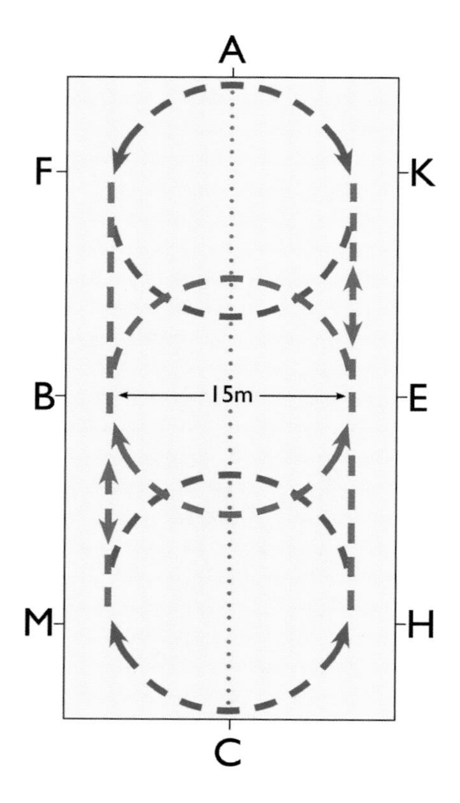

Exercise 1: 15m circles.

EXERCISE 2

Initially on the left rein, lunge your horse on a 20m circle around X (red line). Spiral in (purple line) to a 10m circle (blue line), and out again (green line). Aim for collected steps on the smaller circle, and lengthened strides on the larger circle. This can be done in walk, trot and canter on both reins.

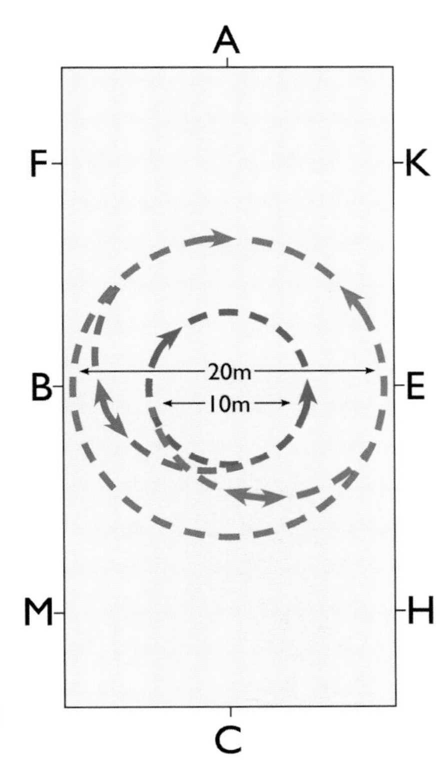

Exercise 2: Spiralling in from a 20m circle, and out again.

Common lungeing problems and solutions

Your horse turns in at you when you ask him to halt

This often happens when trying to ask your horse to halt too far away from you. It is much easier to spiral him in so he ends up halting by your shoulder. Here you have much more control over keeping him straight in the halt. Start him off in 'close up lungeing position' to send him out on the circle again. Correct this issue with in-hand work (see page 66).

Incorrect flexion

The horse looking to the outside when being lunged goes hand-in-hand with your horse falling in on a circle. An untrained horse will tend to look to the outside when turning circles in canter. Through training, he will learn to bend through his body, and flex in the direction of the canter lead. However, if he bends more to the outside on one rein than the other, this can be a sign of stiffness. As the horse's muscles develop through training, he will gradually improve in his balance and suppleness, so he can bend and flex correctly. It is important to take time so that the horse relaxes in his work and not to force him, which would create tension, only making him more resistant and stiff.

Attach the lunge rein through the bit to the roller to encourage better flexion to the inside. Make sure the size of circle is not too small. It should be large enough so your horse remains in 'four-wheel drive' and is not going around 'on two wheels' with all his weight on his inside fore and hind leg.

Lungeing with the lunge rein passed through the bit and fastened to the roller can help with flexion issues. It is also useful if your horse has previously learnt to pull away from you on the lunge, as it makes turning him on to a circle much easier, with less resistance.

Pulling away, breaking free

Lungeing with the lunge rein passed through the bit and fastened to the roller is also useful if your horse has previously learnt to pull away from you on the lunge, as it makes turning him on to a circle much easier, with less resistance.

If the horse tries to pull away, use the line to bring the horse's head towards you so that he has to bend, and cannot shoot off. Once he relaxes, and calms down, soften the rein so his head is straight again.

Remedial work

The following exercises can be used to improve existing issues.

Uneven strides

Moving with shorter steps on one side of the body, or with one fore or hind limb, is a sign of crookedness and can be a symptom of restricted back movement. Use side-reins to maintain a correctly rounded outline. Have the side-reins the same length and low enough so that your horse works through his back. Having his neck high and short, either on the lunge or ridden, will affect the evenness and expression of his strides in all gaits. Try to walk and trot in as slow a tempo as possible, at a snail's pace in fact, to give your horse a chance to place his feet in a clear rhythm. Should your horse stop, or break from trot to walk, calmly use this as a transition, and correct your horse's balance with a couple of half-halts on the lunge rein before resuming the walk or trot. Once this rhythm is clear and he is relaxed, increase the tempo so he works with more energy. If you chase him on in your desperation to get him 'going forwards' he will panic and become tense, reverting to uneven strides as his 'default mode'. Canter work can be introduced once your horse works rhythmically and with even strides in a slower or quicker tempo in walk and trot.

Hollowing

If your horse goes around with his head in the air with a hollow back and his hind legs trailing, his back will be weak, and he will have an overdeveloped muscle under his neck. If this is so, he will have difficulty stretching down. This can be rectified by lungeing him in a Chambon, encouraging the development of the topline muscles. It will take about a month for the new muscle to build, and the muscle under the neck to diminish.

Overbending

If your horse overbends in an effort to avoid contact with the bit, there are a couple of methods of rectifying this. One is to lunge him in the Chambon to encourage him to reach forwards and downwards to the bit rather than looking at his knees. Many people think that 'stretching' involves having the nose behind the vertical but, in my opinion, the horse is only truly stretching if his nose is in front of the vertical with a relaxed and open poll joint. Horses who are overbent often have weak muscles just in front of the withers, seen as a dip in the neck, and overdeveloped bulky muscles at the top of the neck, where the neck bends falsely a short distance behind the poll, instead of at the poll. A horse who stretches truly 'forwards and downwards' is evenly muscled along his topline, flexes at the poll and works with his nose on, or just in front of, the vertical and moves in balance, with his hind legs taking weight under his body.

Once he is able to stretch, he can learn to work into the contact correctly. By using just one side-rein on the outside, and having the lunge rein attached directly to the bit on the inside, you can keep his neck in the correct position with small half-halts, keeping the contact still and light when he gets the idea, so he learns to accept the contact, flexes at the poll and, with his nose on or just in front of the vertical, works into the outside side-rein.

Crookedness

The Chambon is also very useful for correcting crookedness. Simply by encouraging the horse to stretch fully to the ground, he will learn to straighten his whole spine. If your horse is tight through his poll (especially if he has restricted movement on one side of his neck), by loosening the poll joint fully, the whole spine relaxes and your horse will straighten through his neck. Ensure your horse can step evenly in walk before attempting trot.

The Chambon is very useful for correcting crookedness. Simply by encouraging your horse to stretch fully to the ground, he will learn to straighten his poll. Here, the poll is slightly crooked, but by loosening that particular joint fully, the whole spine relaxes and the horse straightens.

Tension

If your horse gets a bit lively, it is important to move around the school with him rather than hauling him around on a small circle. Once he has calmed down, work can begin. If the horse has a lot of energy, sometimes he can surprise you with amazing steps. Using the whole school keeps the horse working in balance, which will help him to relax and settle. Working on a small circle will make him stressed and he may well try to get away from you.

If your horse gets a bit lively, it is important to move around the school with him rather than hauling him around on a small circle. Once he has calmed down, work can begin. If the horse has a lot of energy, sometimes he can surprise you with amazing steps. Here is a lovely moment of suspension in the canter!

Loading problems

It may sound odd to say that lungeing your horse will help with loading issues, but it really does work. If a horse is tense he will raise his head, and may rear or run backwards. However, if he is relaxed he will lower his neck, so if your horse is used to being lunged in a Chambon, and has learnt to stretch forwards and downwards, this can help him to lower his neck and relax, so he walks calmly into the trailer, or lorry. As a training exercise, have your trailer or lorry close by parked in an enclosed area. First lunge your horse until he is calm and listening to you, then lead him in and out of the trailer/ lorry a few times, making sure he halts and stands quietly inside before leading him out again.

Above left Some horses raise their head high when presented with a trailer to go into, and may rear up. Using a Chambon, provided the horse is used to being lungeing in one, and has learnt to stretch forwards and downwards, can help to lower his neck and relax, so he walks calmly into the trailer, or lorry.

Above right Once the horse has relaxed, the Chambon loosens, and Amadeus walks calmly up the ramp.

Right Walking through the trailer and out the other end as a training exercise, so Amadeus remains relaxed on exiting the trailer. Of course, this is just a training exercise. I would not travel a horse wearing a Chambon – I would remove it before travel, though ideally I would not go to a show until the loading issue was sorted out!

CHAPTER SIX

Long-reining

LONG-REINING CAN either be done on a circle as you would when lungeing (double-lungeing) or you can be behind your horse as you would when driving. Long-reining and double-lungeing can be done from a lunge cavesson, with a young horse or one who cannot tolerate a bit for whatever reason, or from the bit. A lunge whip can be used for either double-lungeing or long-reining, although you may prefer a long schooling whip, or piaffe whip, if you find a lunge whip too much to cope with. If your horse is obedient to you on the lunge, you may not need a whip at all! When long-reining behind your horse, a lunge whip may be useful if your horse is likely to kick out, so you can stay far enough away from him to be out of range of his hind legs!

Long-reining on a circle (double-lungeing)

Double-lungeing enables you to be in control of the rein contact as though you were riding your horse on a circle. There are various ways the reins can be used for different effects. When changing direction, you will have to bring your horse to a halt and alter the long-reins accordingly. Using long-reins that clip on to the roller rather than threading through the rings makes changing the positioning of the reins quick and easy.

The first stage of double-lungeing follows on from lungeing with the lunge rein to the bit and the outside side-rein attached as described earlier. Have the inside rein attached to the bit and the outside rein passing over your horse's back. Use the reins as though you were riding, keeping an even contact on both reins with your hands in 'riding position'.

Double-lungeing with the inside rein attached to the bit and the outside rein over the horse's back. Use the reins as though you were riding, keeping an even contact on both. This is the first stage of double-lungeing, and follows on from lungeing with the outside side-rein attached as described earlier.

The next stage is with the inside rein passing from the roller, through the bit to your hand, and the outside rein over the horse's back. The inside rein helps to maintain flexion, and makes it easy for you to turn your horse, especially if he should he try to dash off. Keep an even contact with both the inside and outside rein at all times. The inside rein is to encourage correct flexion, not to pull the horse's head around.

To get your horse used to having the outside rein behind his haunches requires a bit of preparatory work in the stable – getting him used to being touched on the hind legs with a lead rope, for example, or wearing a rug with

Double-lungeing with the inside rein passing from the roller, through the bit to my hand, and the outside rein over the back. The inside rein helps to maintain flexion, and makes it easy for me to turn Norman should he try to dash off.

Keep an even contact with both the inside and outside rein at all times. The inside rein is to encourage correct flexion, not to pull the horse's head around!

a back strap around his haunches. If he is used to this, there should be no problem with having the rein behind him. Attach the inside rein directly to the bit and have the outside rein around the haunches to encourage your horse to step under his body.

The reason for attaching the inside rein directly to the bit when introducing the outside rein behind the haunches is to make sure the horse remains relaxed. The focus here is primarily on the engagement of the hind legs. It is important not to 'shorten the neck' in an effort to make the horse 'rounder'. Once your horse takes more weight behind, and lowers his haunches, he will arch his neck as a result of lifting his back.

Above left Here, I have the inside rein attached directly to the bit and the outside rein around the haunches to encourage Norman to step under his body.

Above right The rein around the haunches should not be pulled tight, but just taut enough to keep it lightly against the hind legs so it does not drop down below the hocks.

Left Working with the outside rein behind the haunches. It is important not have it too tight or too loose. Allow your horse to bend around the circle. Here, Norman is working in a relaxed manner, with his neck forwards, a good starting point, but I am not asking him to engage his haunches.

Working with the inside rein attached to the roller and passing through the inside bit ring, and the outside rein behind the hind legs to encourage engagement.

Once your horse works happily with the outside rein behind him, you can ask for more engagement with frequent half-halts and transitions either within the gaits, or between them. If you need to improve your horse's flexion, you can attach the inside rein to the roller, passing it through the inside bit ring as mentioned earlier.

To summarize the progression when double-lungeing, it is as follows:

1. Inside rein directly to the bit, outside rein over the back.
2. Inside rein attached to the roller, passing through the bit, and the outside rein over the horse's back.
3. Inside rein directly to the bit, and the outside rein behind.
4. Inside rein attached to the roller, passing through the bit, and the outside rein behind.

It is very important not to get into a pulling match with your horse. Maintain a light contact with the bit and guide him around the school. Use straight lines as well as circles, positioning yourself as for lungeing. Because the reins are very long, they are heavier than the bridle reins, so lightness is the key. The advantage of double-lungeing as opposed to using side-reins is that you can allow your horse to stretch forwards and down by easing the reins, and take the reins up again to work him into the contact. There is no need to detach or re-attach them. Allow your horse to stretch frequently during a training session for a good gymnastic workout.

Keeping a correct contact with the double lunge. Guide the horse, do not pull him.

Allow the horse to stretch fully down to the ground with his nose forwards and downwards at frequent intervals to make sure he is really relaxed, both mentally physically.

Right Working through the back with a lowered neck position. Note that Norman's nose is correctly in front of the vertical, reaching forwards to the bit, as I encourage him to step under behind with the outside rein behind his haunches. You should see your horse's back muscles working – they look like long bands running along where the saddle would be. You should also notice his abdominal muscles tightening as he brings each hind leg forwards.

Double-lungeing exercises to try

All gaits can be used whichever way you have the long-reins attached. With the rein behind the haunches, more engagement can be asked for by half-halting frequently. Transitions between the gaits can be greatly improved with double-lungeing. The following are two exercises to try.

EXERCISE 1

Starting on the left rein at A, make 12m circles to the left (blue line), then at the middle point of the long side at B (green line), at C (blue line) and on the next long side at E (purple line). Travel straight on the track (red line) from one circle to the next. Repeat on the other rein.

EXERCISE 2

Starting at A on the left rein, go around the track (purple line) to C. At C, on a 15 m circle (blue line), make transitions between walk and trot. Proceed on the track around to A (purple line) and on a 20m circle (red line), make canter-walk-canter transitions. Repeat on the right rein.

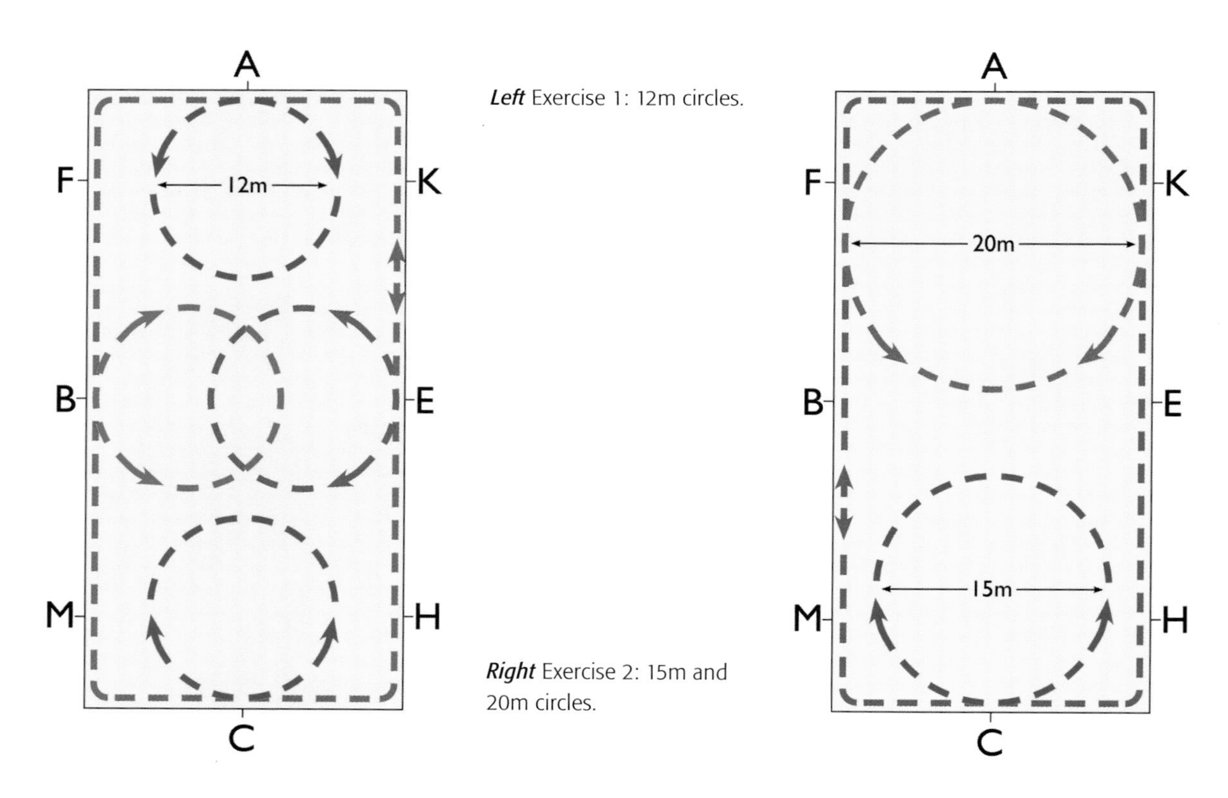

Left Exercise 1: 12m circles.

Right Exercise 2: 15m and 20m circles.

Common double-lungeing problems and solutions

Correct height and tension of reins

When working with the outside rein behind the haunches, it is important not to have it too tight. If you do, the rein may slip upwards under your horse's tail, which may cause him to clamp his tail and speed off! Conversely, if the rein is too loose, it may drop below his hocks and he may step over it. Aim to keep the rein just above his hocks at all times. On a circle, the outside rein must allow your horse to bend around the circle. Having it too tight means that your horse cannot bend and may become tense.

Difficulties associated with using two separate reins

The difficulties that this presents are common to both double-lungeing and long-reining on straight lines, and are discussed later in this chapter (see page 123).

Overbending

If your horse overbends, stick with having the inside rein directly to the bit and have the outside rein over his back until he relaxes into the contact and can stretch forwards into it. Once he takes his nose forwards into the contact rather than looking at his knees and avoiding it, he will work through his back, with his hind legs taking weight. Aim to correct the whole horse, rather than just focusing on his neck position. As he gets stronger through his back and abdomen, his head and neck carriage will improve.

Remedial work

The following exercises can be used to improve existing issues.

Crookedness and incorrect flexion

These issues can be greatly improved on the double-lunge. Using the reins with the inside rein passed through the inside bit ring to the roller, and the other rein behind the haunches, make changes of flexion to the inside, and to the outside, making sure to straighten the horse in between. Be aware that swinging his neck from side to side will just unbalance him and weaken the muscles at the base of his neck. All you need to do is to turn his ears one way, straighten them, and then turn them the other way – to the inside of the circle, and to the outside – true flexion and counter-flexion.

Tightness through the back/hind legs trailing

With the line behind the haunches, use the contact with both reins to help the horse to 'sit' in transitions. Lighten the contact as soon as he has tucked his loins under. If the haunches take weight properly, the neck will arch forwards correctly to the bit. Frequent transitions will help your horse to work through his back, which in turn will bring his hind legs under his body.

Long-reining on straight lines

Long-reining on straight lines is the nearest thing to riding your horse without actually being in the saddle! The aim is to be directly behind your horse so he cannot see you, but can hear your voice and feel your body aids through the rein contact, but initially you may need to give your horse confidence that you are still there by being slightly to one side so he can see you. Move behind him for a few steps at a time, talking to him, and maintaining a steady contact at all times. He should feel no difference in your rein contact wherever you are. Long-reining is not about pulling to stop and letting go to move him forwards. It is about co-ordination of your reins, whip, body and voice.

Attach the reins so they pass from the bit rings, to the roller, and to your hands. In this way, it is easy to make changes of direction without having to alter the reins in any way.

When long-reining in the school, you can use all the school movements that you can ride! Working behind your horse will be done in walk, although if your horse can maintain a steady collected trot and canter, you should be able to keep up! If you cannot keep up, trot and canter work can always be done on a circle and interspersed with movements in walk. This can help to refresh the walk, and also to relax the horse should he get a bit tense at any time. Collecting the walk should be achieved with half-halts. To extend the walk, ease the rein contact and allow your horse to take bigger, more ground-covering steps. Do remember that you will have to collect and lengthen your own steps to match your horse's strides!

Walking straight on the long side behind Norman. His attention is fully on me even though he cannot see me.

You must be able to keep your horse straight, even when walking to one side so he can see you.

Good relaxation from both me and Heinrich long-reining confidently in the field.

Above left Changing the rein on the diagonal.

Above right Medium walk on the long side.

Left Lengthening the walk steps into extended walk.

Below left A lovely balanced trot. If you cannot keep up behind your horse, move beside him so you can bring him around on a circle if necessary.

Below right A few moments in canter on a circle can relieve tension!

Working on flexion and bend

Long-reining your horse is a great opportunity to perfect his flexion and bend, positioning him to the right and to the left. This is preparatory work for circles and turns as well as for lateral movements. Make sure you can see his ears and that he is straight to start with. From behind, you can see if your horse bends equally to the right and to the left. If you cannot see his ears, he is overbent! Correct his outline with half-halts. As he takes weight behind, his ears will come back into view. To flex your horse to the right, turn your body in the direction you want him to bend. Use your whole body rather than just the reins. If you give rein aids that are too strong, your horse will become tense.

When long-reining on circles, it may help to use a pole on the ground as a focal point. When making turns and circles, it can also help to imagine you are in the rear carriage of a train, with your horse at the front. This ensures that you follow the same line as your horse. If you

Above Positioning Heinrich to my left.

Left Positioning Heinrich to my right.

move to one side he will drift the opposite way from you. Keep your hands parallel and with an even contact on both reins. Turn your hips and shoulders in the direction you want your horse to go and look in the direction of his ears. Keep your weight equal on both feet as you turn and avoid leaning into the turn.

Above Circling around a pole as a focal point. ***Right*** If you lose control over the direction your horse is going in, get behind him as soon as you can! You need to be the 'back of the train' with him at the 'front of the train!'

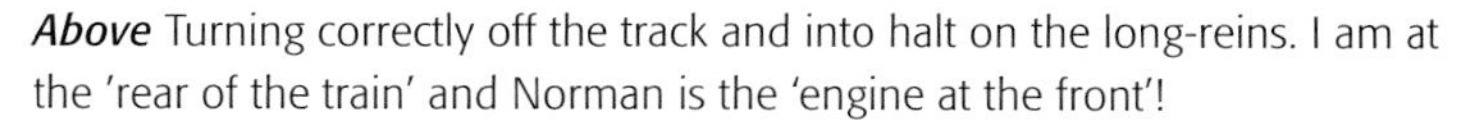

Above Turning correctly off the track and into halt on the long-reins. I am at the 'rear of the train' and Norman is the 'engine at the front'!

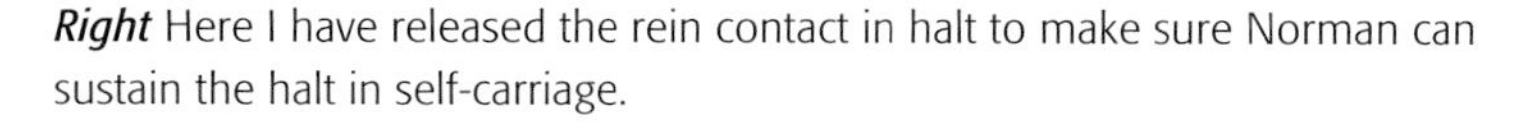

Right Here I have released the rein contact in halt to make sure Norman can sustain the halt in self-carriage.

Piaffe and passage

Once your horse can halt, half-halt and collect in the walk and trot, training for piaffe can begin. From the halt, proceed in a collected walk, and ask for a few piaffe steps by touching your horse on his hind legs with the whip in the same way as when working in hand. Bring him back to halt ready to repeat a few times. Correct your horse's outline with half-halts – remember if the ears disappear, he is dropping his poll!

Passage can be developed from the piaffe. Allow the piaffe steps to travel forwards, touching your horse on the croup with the whip, which helps to encourage the 'bounce' in the passage steps as the steps become more elevated.

Norman in piaffe. He is in a rounded outline, but his poll is rather low.

Asking Norman to step forwards into the beginnings of passage raises his neck.

Long-reining exercises to try

EXERCISE 1

Set out two cones to go between, at about 2m apart (orange spots), round the school near A, B, C and E. Walk from one set of cones to the next (red line), halting between the cones, and walk on again.

You could also rein-back between the obstacles or try a few steps of collection before proceeding, or a few steps of piaffe.

EXERCISE 2

Place two cones (orange spots) either side of X about 2m apart. Using the whole school, starting at A, leave the track at F and go straight to X between the markers (red line). Return to the track at M. Repeat on the next long side, leaving the track at H and returning to K. Repeat on the other rein.

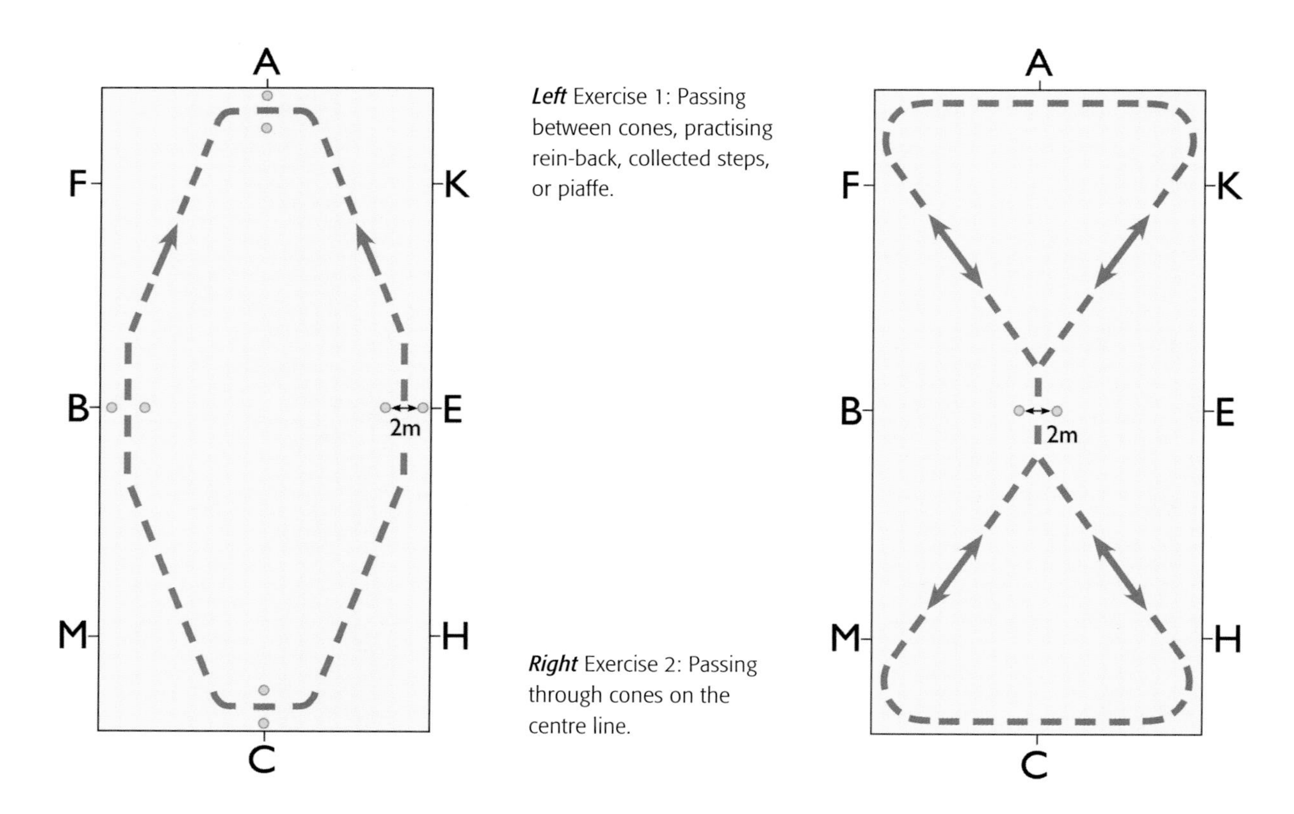

Left Exercise 1: Passing between cones, practising rein-back, collected steps, or piaffe.

Right Exercise 2: Passing through cones on the centre line.

Common long-reining problems and solutions

Double-lungeing and long-reining with two lunge reins

You may have tried long-reining with two separate lunge reins. This requires the lunge reins to be threaded through the roller rings and can take time, and can also be difficult with a fidgety horse who will not stand still. When lungeing on a circle with two separate lines, with both reins passing from the bit, through the roller rings and to your hands, it is much more difficult to maintain an even contact on both reins and harder to adjust the length of each individual rein. It is far easier to use long-reins that buckle together, or a continuous rein, where you have the opportunity to adjust the contact to the inside and outside of the bit as you would when riding. See photos on page 124.

Another issue with two lunge reins is that there is much more of a handful in each hand, and this makes it difficult to handle a whip as well. It all too easy to let one of the reins drop, which the horse can step over. If this happens, you will have to detach one of the lunge reins and place it out of the way so you can disentangle the other from your horse's hind legs. Using a continuous rein and clipping it to the roller makes it much quicker and easier to connect and disconnect rather than going through the fiddly process of threading separate lunge reins through the roller rings. See photos on page 125.

Running back

If your horse runs backwards, this is most probably because you have too strong a contact on the reins. Lighten the rein contact, but without dropping it all together, and go back with the horse, keeping him straight. Avoid panicking – talk to him calmly while maintaining control over your body language and posture so your horse 'stays with you' and doesn't veer off in another direction, so you are turning 'running back' into a controlled 'rein-back'. From this you should be able to halt your horse and let him relax for a moment or two before asking him to walk on. Make a few transitions between walk and halt and end the session on a good note.

Taking off

If your horse takes off or tows you with the reins passing from the bit, to the roller, and then to your hands, attach the inside rein by passing it through

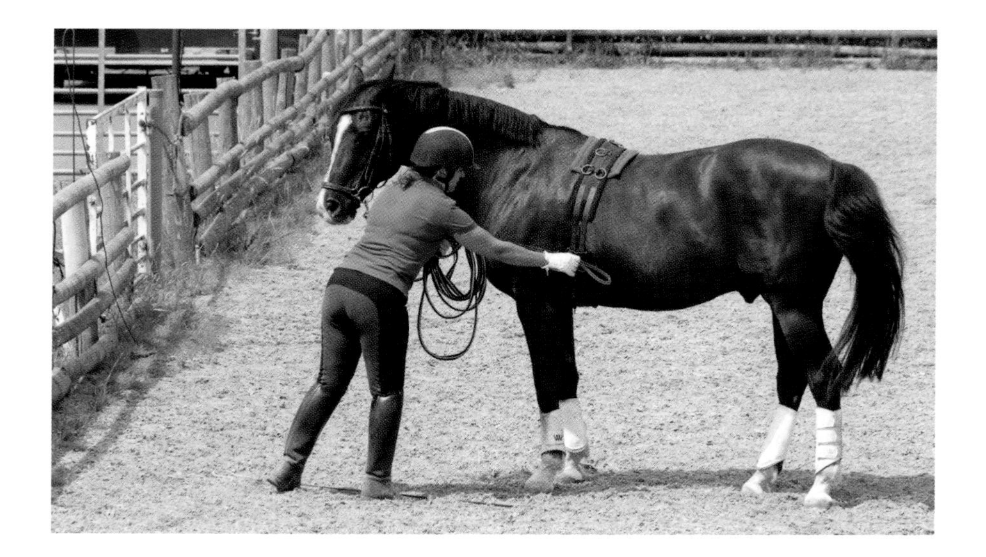

Right Lungeing with two separate lines will necessitate threading each through the roller rings on each side – tricky with a fidgety horse!

Above Ready to long-rein with two separate lines.

Right Lungeing on a circle with two separate lines, with both reins passing from the bit, through the roller rings and to my hands. It is much more difficult to maintain an even contact on both reins like this, and harder to adjust the length of each individual rein.

1. Two lines means more of a handful – in each hand!

2. It is all too easy to let one of the reins drop, which the horse can step over.

3. Here I have detached one of the lunge reins so I can disentangle the other from Norman's hind legs. Norman's 'standing still' training pays off while I sort things out!

4. Ready for the off again.

the inside bit ring then to the roller, as when double-lungeing. This makes it easy to turn the horse on to a circle so you can regain control. Long-reining the horse 'in position', i.e. slightly flexed to the inside, will help him to concentrate. Keep a slow tempo in walk so he has to really think where he is placing his feet. Going 'slightly sideways' like this helps to keep him working into the outside rein, which gives you control, and it is much harder for him to dash off.

Crookedness

If your horse is or becomes crooked, and finds it difficult to walk in a straight line, practise frequent halt transitions to make sure he is using both hind legs equally.

One way of improving a horse's ability to take weight behind is to practise rein-back. However, rein-back can highlight existing crookedness. If your horse becomes crooked in the rein-back, do it between markers such as cones or poles. Make frequent half-halts or transitions to and from halt between obstacles, correcting the halt each time by touching the hind legs with the whip, in the same way as working in hand.

CHAPTER SEVEN

Ground Poles and Cavalletti

POLE AND CAVALLETTI work is excellent for improving your horse's suppleness, co-ordination and balance in all gaits. Use heavy poles which do not roll should your horse touch them.

This work can be done either in hand, on the lunge or on long-reins. You could work over poles in a Chambon or side-reins, or with nothing at all, depending on whether you want to have a relaxing and loosening-up session, or a 'bodybuilding' session in a correctly rounded outline. Always start and finish each session with loosening and stretching work without any side-reins and without going over any poles or cavalletti. If using a Chambon, or doing stretching work where the horse's head is low, stick to ground poles. With cavalletti, you risk the lunge rein getting caught on the supports at either end of the cavalletti. You will need to watch where you are putting your own two feet. It is all too easy to trip over, as you have a lot to concentrate on!

The distances given in this chapter are those I use with my horses, and should suit most, but of course the distances can be adjusted to suit your own horse. Do bear in mind that the striding between poles and cavalletti should encourage the horse to work athletically. Shortening the distances to make life too easy for the horse will not develop him physically or challenge him mentally, but he should not be frightened or asked to do something he is really not capable of.

Ground poles

Start with a single pole in walk or trot. This can be placed anywhere in the school or in the field, but if your horse is likely to run out, put it next to a fence or hedge to act as a 'wing' on the outside. You could also place a couple of ground poles as wings on the inside if needed. Placing four poles in a 'star' formation is a very useful layout, as each pole can be used separately, or you can lunge your horse over them all on a circle. Setting out a couple of options for your schooling session on the lunge provides the facility to do different exercises without having to stop and set things out. When lungeing over poles or cavalletti, make sure you always aim for the centre of each one. Even when working on a circle, keep your horse straight for just a step or two before and after each one, to avoid him 'motorbiking' round the figure.

Start over a single pole in a trot to loosen-up, without any side-reins, etc., with enough energy so your horse steps cleanly over it.

Mr Foley trotting over a single pole in a Chambon.

Norman trotting over a single pole in side-reins on the lunge. The poles are set out in a star shape so Norman trots over them on a circle. Each pole can be used individually also. You can see the cavalletti in the distance. Setting out a couple of patterns for your schooling session on the lunge gives different options to use without having to stop and set them out.

Left and below Norman walks over a single pole on long-reins … and so do I! Working over poles on long-reins means you need to be aware of where you are stepping yourself, as well as your horse!

For in-hand work, poles can be helpful to keep your horse straight when asking for halt. Use a pair of parallel poles set at about 1.5m apart. When positioning your horse to the inside as a preparation for shoulder-in, a couple of poles placed on the long side can help to bring your horse's shoulders away from the fence (see photo).

When using a sequence of poles, start with two and build up to a maximum of six to eight. For trot work, place them at a distance of 1.3m apart. In my experience, contrary to what a lot of riders think, horses I have trained do not jump over two poles as a matter of course. However, if you do have a horse who thinks this is a parallel jump, then use three poles to start with.

Halting between two parallel poles helps to keep Norman straight.

Using poles on the long side to help Norman bring his shoulders off the track in shoulder-in.

1. At the beginning of a row of trotting poles (set at 1.3m apart) make sure have your horse straight at the beginning ...
2. ... and he should still be straight at the end! Aim to keep him over the centre of each pole.

Cavalletti

Cavalletti demand much more from the horse than ground poles. Even at their lowest height, you will notice a big difference in your horse's athleticism. Personally I like to use wooden cavalletti, which do not roll or move when touched. If you prefer you could use poles raised on plastic blocks. As with solid cross-country fences, or logs on the ground, the horse knows the difference between these and poles that move, or jumps that can be knocked down. Cavalletti are great for developing cadence in the trot. The advantage of using cavalletti is that they can easily be set at three different heights off the ground simply by turning them over. (Although it sounds obvious, they all need to be turned in the same direction if the distances between them are to be retained.) The lowest height is suitable for all gaits, the middle height for trot and canter, and the highest for canter only. Going over a sequence of cavalletti just once or twice on each rein is often enough for your horse at one time.

If you are long-reining over cavalletti in walk, do watch where you are putting your feet. If working in trot on long-reins, move to the side so that, when your horse goes over the cavalletti, you do not have to run over them!

Above Walking over cavalletti on long-reins. The cavalletti are set for trot, but unless you are very good at running, it is best to walk over them. Walking over trot distances can teach the horse to look where he is going and to think where he is putting his feet. However, if he is clumsy, it may be better to have a single pole placed elsewhere in the school for him to walk over as a preparatory exercise.

Left Here Norman is trotting over the poles and I have moved to the side so he goes over them and I can run alongside.

To improve your horse's bend and flexion on a turn, place up to four cavalletti in a fan shape in a corner of the school. This is a good exercise for building muscle and strength. The distance between the centre of each is 1.3m for working in trot. For walk distance, set them at 0.8m apart. Aim to go over the centre of each one, maintaining an accurate line through the corner. To work on lengthening the strides, go over the outer side of the cavalletti. To collect the strides, go over the inner side.

Cavalletti are great for improving the canter. Canter over a single one to start with, at its lowest height. For a small grid, for a bounce stride in canter, set three cavalletti at 2.5m apart at their lowest height. These will also be at a suitable distance for walking and trotting over, so are useful for a com-

Trotting over cavalletti in a fan on a corner. Going over the centre of the cavalletti in working trot. This photo and the next were taken a couple of years ago with Norman. You can see in the more recent photos through this book how much he has developed!

Trotting over the outer sides of the cavalletti demands bigger steps from your horse and is a good way to develop medium trot.

plete training session. When walking over them there will be two strides in between each, and in trot one stride in between each. Make sure you carry your lunge rein high enough to clear the cavalletti. It can help to put dressage boards as wings to prevent your rein being caught on the cross ends.

To introduce lungeing over cavalletti in canter, start with just one. Whether to use side-reins or not depends on the individual horse. Personally, I find that using side-reins helps to maintain a correctly rounded outline and to regulate the speed and rhythm of the canter. If your horse is calm and

Right These three cavalletti are set at 2.5m apart – for a bounce stride in canter – but are a suitable distance for walking and trotting over. They are set at their lowest height position here.

Below When trotting over them, there will be one stride in between each.

Make sure you carry your lunge rein high enough to clear the cavalletti. I have used dressage boards as wings to prevent my rein being caught on the cross ends.

The cavalletti are set at their middle height here and Norman is having to trot with more elevation.

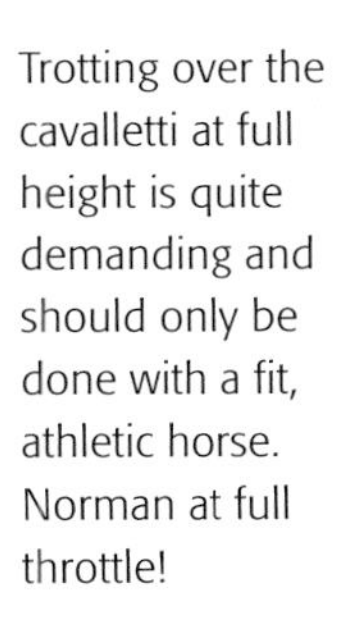

Trotting over the cavalletti at full height is quite demanding and should only be done with a fit, athletic horse. Norman at full throttle!

not likely to make a dash for it, or run out to the side, then do the cavalletti without them. Cantering over cavalletti without side-reins gives the horse the freedom to lengthen his neck as he would over a fence, but as the cavalletti are not very high, this stretch will be minimal. If your horse is inclined to hollow his back when jumping, using side-reins can encourage him to canter with a rounded back.

Cantering over cavalletti is not just preparation for jumping, it also improves the athleticism of the canter stride, and for this reason I think that using side-reins to maintain straightness, rhythm and a correctly rounded outline is helpful. See the sequence of photos overleaf.

1. Approaching the cavalletti in canter, it is so important to start off straight. Norman starts to take off over the first …

2.… followed by a bounce jump over the next, and is really concentrating on what he is doing.

3. Landing on his forefeet in between the last two cavalletti …

4.… and taking off from the hind feet. Norman is in balance as he turns away from the last of the cavalletti to come around on a circle. An alternative would be to continue straight on, but you will have to be a good sprinter to keep up with a horse if you choose this route! It is important not to pull the horse around as he turns. You can see that my lunge rein is there to guide him – it is not tight.

Pole and cavalletti exercises to try

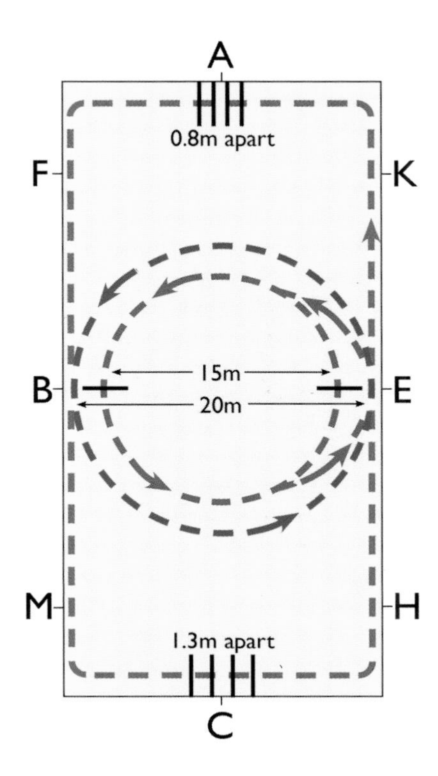

EXERCISE 1

Place four poles at walk distance (about 0.8m apart) at the A end of the school and four poles at trot distance (1.3m) apart at the C end. Place a single pole off the track at B, at right angles to the long side, and another similarly off the track at E. Starting on the left rein (red line), walk over the poles at A; after the corner, trot at F and make a 20m circle going around the poles at B and E (blue line). Trot over the poles at C; at E make a circle of 15m, going over the poles at B and E (purple line) and walk again before the poles at A. Repeat on the other rein. You could circle around or over the poles at E and B in walk, trot or canter. If you do not have this many poles, just set four poles for walk distance at A in one training session and use trot poles at C in the next.

EXERCISE 2

Set four cavalletti out in a fan based on a 15m circle, in the corner of the school at K, with the distance between the centre of each pole 1.3m for working in trot. Trot over them three or four times in each direction (red line), interspersed with working for a few minutes in trot elsewhere in the school on both reins. For walk distance, set them at 0.8m apart. Walk over them up to three times in each direction (red line).

At the C end of the school, place four cavalletti in a star formation based on a 15m circle, with their inner edges at about 10m apart (see diagram). Go over these in walk, trot or canter on both reins (blue line). You could use poles instead of cavalletti if you wish.

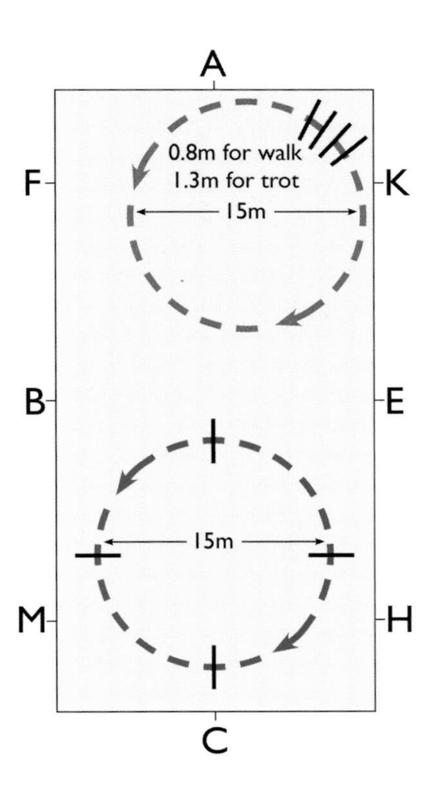

Top diagram Exercise 1: Working over poles and on 15m and 20m circles.

Right Exercise 2: Fan and star exercise.

Problem-solving and remedial work

If your horse panics when faced with a line of poles, go back to using a single one. Once he is relaxed with this, place two or three poles at double trot distance with a step in between (approximately 2.5m apart).

Most problems come from not setting your poles/cavalletti out at the correct distance, or it may be that your lungeing technique needs some improvement. Make sure you always line your horse up with the centre of the poles with sufficient impulsion, but without rushing.

Done correctly, using a series of poles/cavalletti really helps to improve the quality of the gaits – improving rhythm and cadence, straightness and strength through the back.

Bear in mind that this work is quite demanding, so aim to go over your pole/cavalletti layout a maximum of three or four times on each rein and give your horse a break in between for a few minutes, with different work such as transitions between the gaits. Pay great attention to your horse's fitness and state of mind, making sure he enjoys his work at all times and is not overtaxed.

CHAPTER **EIGHT**

Jumping

JUMPING WITHOUT THE rider can either be done on the lunge using a lunge rein attached to a lunge cavesson, or double-lungeing with long-reins from the cavesson or bridle (if you are confident that you will not catch the horse in the mouth), or free-jumping. The horse should jump with no training aids at all, so he has the freedom of his neck over the fence for balance.

Ideally an indoor school is best, as there is no risk of your horse jumping out, but most riders will be working outside, so make sure you do not build fences for your horse that are higher than the school surround. This also applies to jumping in the field – if you are going over cross-country obstacles on the lunge, make sure the area is secure in case you let go!

Lungeing over fences is a great way to teach your horse to jump as it builds his self-confidence and develops his jumping technique, suppleness, and the ability to think for himself. This is a very important aspect of jumping training. If your horse can get himself out of a tricky situation, you can trust him to get *you* out of trouble when riding him over fences. Should you bring him in on a poor approach, or ask him to take off too soon or too late, he should think and react to tackle the obstacle successfully. (That said, this confidence and self-reliance are valuable assets in the horse that should be nurtured carefully – they should never be an excuse for careless riding.) If your horse is brave enough to tackle obstacles on the lunge that are new to him, such as ditches, coloured fillers, water trays, etc., riding him over them will be a breeze, provided you are not nervous, of course!

Introducing jumping in hand

Start by placing plastic blocks as jump wings with a pole on the ground between them. Use poles as wings to prevent your horse from running out. Remember that you will have a lunge rein to cope with, so do not use anything too high that you will not be able to raise the line over! Cavalletti are very useful as small jumps.

Before jumping, it is first important to loosen-up your horse in walk, trot and canter around the school or field.

Above Begin by working your horse in trot around the field or school before jumping to give his muscles a chance to loosen-up and his mind to settle.

Right Loosening-up work over cavalletti with Norman settles him and focuses his mind before jumping.

Begin by leading your horse over the pole on the ground between the blocks. This will reassure him if he is a bit worried at first. Once he can walk over it calmly in both directions, lunge him over it. He will most probably jump over it giving it a lot of room if he is new to jumping. Once he has relaxed and realized that it is just a pole on the ground, he should just trot over it. (If the horse has previously done some pole/cavalletti work, as discussed earlier, this shouldn't be an issue.) Then canter over it three or four times in each direction. Once he has mastered this, build a small fence – no more than 0.5m high (my preference is for a straight pole with another as a ground-line), and approach it from trot. This helps your horse to remain calm and to think about where to take off rather than launching himself at it from a great distance, or cantering at it too quickly.

Lead him over a pole on the ground where the fence will be to get him used to going between the blocks.

Here, Norman is taking off a long way away from the pole, giving it a lot of room.

Keep each training session to about half an hour, with a loosening-up phase of ten minutes, fifteen minutes of work to include trotting over the pole on the ground, cantering over the pole on the ground and jumping two or three times in each direction over a small fence, and five minutes of relaxing and stretching work afterwards. You may only get as far as trotting over the pole calmly in one session. It is far better to build up to a small fence over several short sessions, always finishing on a good note, rather than having one long one with you both ending up tired and stressed. If you hit a problem, go back to the beginning and start again.

Once your horse has understood what is required from him, i.e. to approach a small fence calmly from trot, you can focus on his jumping technique. He may jump cleanly, picking up his feet, or he may trail his legs, just clearing the fence. He should work it out for himself. If he hits the pole, he may panic and shoot forwards. If this happens, run with him, and gradually bring him back under control on a large circle at first, gradually spiralling in to a smaller one in trot, then an even smaller one in walk, and end up with him halting close to you. This is a safe way to bring your horse back under control and keeps his concentration on you. Once he approaches the fence calmly in trot and jumps with a nicely rounded topline (a good bascule), practise bringing him in from a steady canter.

A lovely rounded shape, a bascule, in the air.

Make sure you always bring your horse in straight on the approach, and keep him straight for a few strides afterwards. Quite often, the horse will want to turn sharply after the fence. This is to be discouraged by using wings, or poles on the ground alongside the fence, and by moving on a straight line with him. Avoid pulling him around as this could unbalance him.

In order to keep him straight, you will need to run alongside your horse as he jumps. Raise your lunge rein as he takes off to make sure you do not restrict the freedom of his neck over the fence, and to make sure it does not get caught up on the wings.

Keep your horse straight over the fence so he can make a balanced take-off from both hind feet at once.

You will need to run alongside your horse as he jumps in order to keep him straight. Raise your lunge rein as he takes off to make sure it does not get caught up on the wings, and that you do not restrict the freedom of his neck over the fence.

Above left On the approach in canter, Mr Foley is concentrating on where to take off.

Above right Young or inexperienced horses often jump big. Make sure you raise the lunge rein as he jumps.

Left A lovely straight landing. Avoid pulling your horse around sharply after a fence as this will unbalance him. Move forwards with him on a straight line. You may need to run fast!

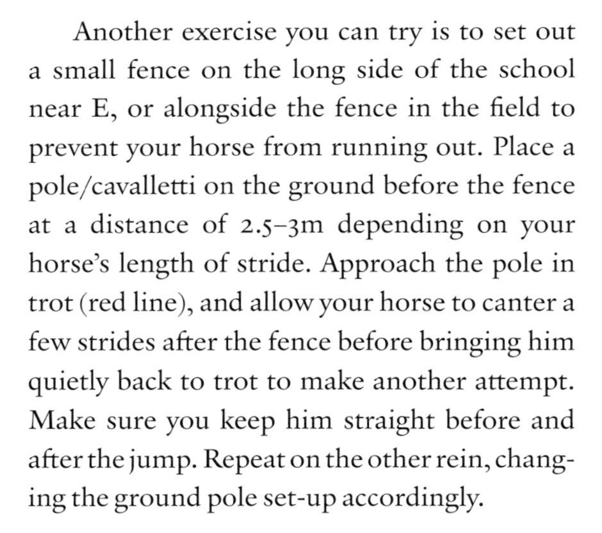

Another exercise you can try is to set out a small fence on the long side of the school near E, or alongside the fence in the field to prevent your horse from running out. Place a pole/cavalletti on the ground before the fence at a distance of 2.5–3m depending on your horse's length of stride. Approach the pole in trot (red line), and allow your horse to canter a few strides after the fence before bringing him quietly back to trot to make another attempt. Make sure you keep him straight before and after the jump. Repeat on the other rein, changing the ground pole set-up accordingly.

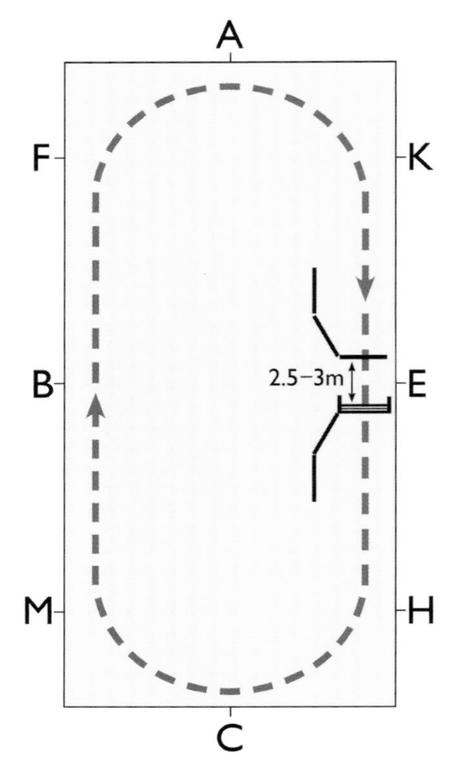

Jumping exercise.

With a more experienced horse, you can build a bounce obstacle by placing a cavalletti at 3.5m before the fence. Start with it at its lowest height to make sure the distance suits the horse before raising it to the middle height, followed by placing it at the highest setting. This helps the horse to develop power and strength as he has to land and take off again straight away. It teaches him to think quickly and improves his co-ordination. The main fence should be between about 0.75–1m high. The idea here is to give the horse gymnastic work to improve the suppleness of his spine and dexterity, not to put him under pressure by seeing how high he can jump.

Above left Norman jumps over the cavalletti placed at its fullest height at a distance of 3.5m in front of the fence.

Above right Landing and taking off straight away in this 'bounce jump' where Norman has to bring his hind legs right under his body.

Left A lovely bascule over the fence which is 0.75m high. His withers are the highest point.

Gridwork on the lunge really improves the horse's ability to lift his forehand and tuck his legs up over a fence. With a correct bascule, the horse's withers should be the highest point in mid-air, with the neck stretched forwards and downwards, and the haunches tucked under. Sounds familiar? This takes us back to the very beginning of the book, with correct stretching work – with the nose reaching forwards and downwards, the back and abdominal muscles engaged, and the haunches tucked under, with the hind legs taking weight under the body.

Besides jumping your horse on a single lunge rein, another option is to jump him using the double-lunge. This gives you a bit more control over his jumping technique – use the reins exactly as you would from the saddle. You can use half-halts to control the trot or canter on the approach, and also keep

Gridwork on the lunge really improves the horse's ability to tuck his legs up over a fence. Here Norman lifts his shoulders and tucks his forefeet neatly under to clear the fence.

Jumping on the double lunge. Use the reins as you would when jumping from the saddle – allow the horse to stretch his neck forwards over the fence. Make sure that you raise your hands as he jumps to follow the arc of his movement and so that the reins don't get caught on the wings. Using the double-lunge is very useful to keep the horse straight as he jumps, and gives you the chance to balance him with half-halts before and after the fence.

him straight after the fence by using your reins as though you were riding. Make sure you allow him to stretch forwards with his neck over the fence.

If you free-jump your horse over fences, make sure that your fences are lower than whatever surrounds the school, and place the fence(s) in the middle of the long side so there is no risk of him assuming you want him to jump out of the school. An indoor school is a safer option, if you have access to one.

Mr Foley free-jumping in the school. Using poles as wings helps to keep him straight.

Common jumping problems and solutions

Too fast/too slow

Most problems jumping on the lunge stem from a poor approach – coming in too fast, whereby your horse flattens over the fence and may knock it with his forefeet, or too slowly, whereby the take-off is laboured and the hind feet do not have enough push to clear the fence, so the horse knocks it behind. In either case, spend some time with lunge work to improve his balance and attention before going back to the beginning of jump training and lungeing him over a ground pole. Only jump again once he has calmed down.

If your horse has no energy in his jumping, ask yourself if this is a confidence issue, or a laziness problem. In either case, go back to basic lunge work and use transitions to get him more balanced. As he takes more weight behind, he should develop more 'pushing power' to get up in the air.

Crooked take-off

If your horse jumps crookedly, the solution is down to you bringing him in straight to the fence, so work on your own technique! Note, however, that the horse may be stronger on one side of his body, and have more thrust from one hind leg than the other, in which case it is important to work him on both reins so he develops more evenly through his body. Make sure that you bring him in from a large circle and give him plenty of time to be straight before and after the fence. Keep him steady – too much speed can result in him 'motorbiking' into the fence.

A combination of poles, cavalletti and small fences is extremely good gymnastic work for your horse and is fun for him, doing as much good for him mentally as physically. A session once a week is really beneficial for all disciplines. It adds variety to your horse's work regime, and is a good way to improve his bravery and self-confidence.

CHAPTER **NINE**

Lungeing the Rider

So FAR, THIS BOOK has dealt with working the horse from the ground using lungeing, long-reining and in-hand techniques. However, lungeing is, of course, also a very useful means of developing a rider's posture and feel so I'd like to round things off by looking at lungeing from this perspective.

Suitability of the horse

The horse used for the lunge lesson must absolutely trust the trainer. Within commonsense boundaries and assuming physical capabilities, the horse's age is immaterial, but it is usually the case that an older horse who is well established in his work will cope better than a less experienced horse. One aspect related to this is that I know, from experience, that an old, wise horse can be as canny as a barrowload of monkeys, and refuse to move at all unless the rider is sitting perfectly in the saddle with total humility! To me, this is the true schoolmaster horse.

One factor that can complicate the issue for the instructor is that it is usually easier to lunge a rider on their own horse. A rider can be anxious on a different horse, and is more likely to be relaxed on their own. In such a case it is incumbent upon the instructor to establish a rapport with both horse and rider – but this can be easier than familiarizing

It takes a special horse to be a schoolmaster.

Before the lesson begins, it can be helpful if the rider lunges their own horse to help them both to relax and to get in the right frame of mind for the lesson.

the rider with a strange horse. So, if you train your horse on the lunge, as described in Chapter 5, you simplify the process of having lunge lessons for yourself!

The instructor

The instructor who gives lunge lessons must have patience and awareness and take time to explain what the aims are before the lesson begins, and be prepared to give further clarification during the lesson as and when necessary. A short rest can help the rider (and horse) to relax and is far more effective for developing confidence than going round and around with the rider becoming too tired to concentrate. The length of the lesson should be about 45 minutes, depending on the level of fitness of the rider, and their concentration span.

Handling a horse on the lunge with a rider on board is actually quite hard work, and mentally demanding. The instructor has to keep the horse under control, as well as teaching the rider – so 'two brains' are needed – one for the horse, and one for the rider! In an ideal situation, it is extremely helpful to have a second person who can lead or lunge the horse so the instructor can concentrate on the rider.

The instructor who gives lunge lessons must have patience and awareness and take time to explain what the aims are before the lesson begins.

Helping the rider with their own horse with side-reins attached, and the rider with rein contact. This enables Lorraine with Merlin to concentrate on her position with me as 'back-up' on the ground.

Equipment and preparation

Preparing the horse

- The horse should be in a bridle, a lunge cavesson, saddle, side-reins and leg protection.
- The rider's reins can be either attached to the bit, or to the side rings on the lunge cavesson.
- The instructor can either lunge the horse from the lunge cavesson, or from the bit should the rider need assistance in keeping the horse correctly on the contact.

Prior to starting the lesson, the horse should be warmed up on the lunge, initially without the side-reins attached, to allow him to stretch forwards and downwards, and to get rid of any cheekiness. The side-reins are then attached so the horse loosens up through his back and is working happily into the reins.

Ready for the lesson. Norman is wearing a lunge cavesson with the bridle underneath with the noseband removed.

Loosening up the horse before the rider mounts is important. The horse needs to work happily into the side-reins before the rider gets on board. Here the side-reins are long to encourage Norman to work in a relaxed manner for the rider, rather than to school Norman, in which case they would be a bit shorter.

Assessing and preparing the rider

The instructor should make various assessments of the rider prior to the rider mounting. It may be that the instructor has previously given the rider lessons off the lunge, in which case various strengths and weaknesses will already be known but, if not, a brief conversation can provide useful information.

Either way, attention should be given to the following points.

Posture

A rider can adopt a fair approximation of their riding posture on the ground and this can be assessed and improved before they mount, so that once they are in the saddle they understand how to sit in an upright position.

Contact

Depending on the horse and the level of the rider, the rider may start/have the lesson with or without reins, and the reins may be attached either to the bit or the lunge cavesson. (With an unfamiliar pupil, assessment of their posture may provide clues about likely contact, because a rider who is unlikely to sit quietly in the saddle is unlikely to achieve quiet, consistent contact.)

Calmness, confidence and breathing

These factors are often inter-related.

Without going into all the ins and outs of the rider's day, the instructor should check for circumstances that the pupil may be currently worried about, which might invoke tension rather than calmness. (This discussion should remain focused on the lesson, rather than the pupil's life history.)

Regarding underlying confidence, the pupil may have had a bad experience that makes them nervous about the lesson and affects their confidence. It is important that the instructor finds out about any such event before the lesson, in order to teach accordingly.

Finally – and especially if anything surfaces from the preceding enquiries – the rider should be encouraged to breathe normally. When nerves kick in, many people breathe shallowly – and some forget to breathe when concentrating really hard on trying to get something right.

If this goes on for too long, they may feel faint – which not ideal in a riding lesson. Instructors should make sure they have their first aid certificate up to date!

The rider's perspective

Since, in this chapter, I am encouraging you, the reader, to have lessons on the lunge, I am going to address the following text to you personally. The most beneficial aspect of lunge lessons is to give you the opportunity to concentrate on yourself. It can be a shock to the system, though, to realize that many of your horse's problems are actually yours, which can be a very humbling experience. A lunge lesson is quite intensive, as it pinpoints small details in your riding that can be improved upon. It is working on these small details that can turn a good rider into a great rider!

Position in the saddle

You do not need a load of fancy exercises to help you to develop a secure seat and effective aids – just time and the opportunity to develop balance and feel, which working on the lunge with an instructor can give you. The instructor can keep the horse at a steady speed and rhythm, allowing you to concentrate on yourself and to learn how a correct gait should feel. If you feel unbalanced when going into trot, for example, it is a good idea to hold on to the front of the saddle or use a balance strap attached to the D rings.

Once you are sitting in a good position, with your hips upright, and core muscles toned, you need to concentrate on the movement of your hips and back. In walk, being the slowest gait, you have time to develop awareness of how the horse's back movement affects your own. The middle of your back must move in a controlled manner. Your abdominal muscles should be toned to control this back movement.

Your hips should move with the horse's back, 'right, left, right, left' as he moves each hind leg in turn. This applies to the walk, trot and canter. Your spine must also move to allow the horse to 'swing through the back'. This movement is a ripple through the spine, starting from the lumbar area, and filtering up to your neck. It is important to allow your back to move with the swing of the horse's back, so the horse moves you rather than you making massive movements of your own accord with your back or seat without any co-ordination with the horse's movement. Any stiffness in the spine will have an effect on the freedom of movement of the horse.

Establish a correct position in halt without reins and stirrups before proceeding in walk or trot.

Once you feel confident to do so, you can proceed first in walk, and then go into trot or canter. Riding without reins and stirrups is the best way to develop a good seat.

Your hip, knee and ankle joints also accommodate the horse's movement, while your head, arms, hands and shoulders remain still.

Exercises to develop your back movement

In walk, feel how the horse's back moves yours. Slow down the walk with your hips and back, closing your legs as you do so, to 'hold' the walk at the speed you wish to go. Then, increase the speed a bit with your hips and allow the walk to speed up with your back. The length of stride can also be adjusted by your hip and back movement. Your instructor will help you to find the optimum walk from which to make a transition into trot by teaching you how to alter both the speed and the length of stride.

In trot, allow the swing of the horse's back to move your spine. Think of 'doing the same trot as the horse', rather than just being a passenger. Moving with the horse is about teamwork. Do yourself what you are asking him to do. On the lunge, your instructor can help you to co-ordinate your movement with your horse's.

In canter, many riders push the horse along with their seat in an effort to 'go with the movement', or in an effort to keep the horse going. It is worrying that many riders are taught to do this in their lessons. This 'polishing the saddle' with the seat, pressing into the horse's back, causes the horse's back to hollow, the hind legs to disengage and his head to raise. If the rider concentrates on stretching up through the spine with every canter stride on the 'up' phase (period of suspension), the horse will be able to lift his back, arch his neck and bring his hind legs under his body. On the lunge, the instructor can keep the horse in a correct outline, with the help of correctly fitting side-reins, and keep the canter steady enough for you to sit quietly in the saddle, and feel how the horse moves.

Leg exercises

Leg aids do not just ask the horse to go forwards – they also play a part in controlling the horse, altering his speed, and collecting and lengthening the strides. A secure leg position also helps you to maintain your balance in the saddle. These exercises can be done in walk, trot, or canter.

To establish a correct leg position (with stirrups) first let your legs hang down against the horse's sides, with the soles of your boots parallel to the ground. The weight of your legs should rest on the balls of your feet, on the stirrups, with the hip, knee and ankle joints softly flexed.

Lift your lower legs away from the horse's sides, keeping your knees and thighs on the saddle for security and to maintain the horse's rhythm and balance. Be aware of the lack of contact with your calves. Close your lower legs again and feel the difference. Your upper calves should be in the correct place on the horse to give the aids to 'go forwards' and to 'step under' with the hind legs.

First, establish a correct leg position. Let your legs hang down against the horse's sides, with the soles of your boots parallel to the ground.

With both hands on your hips, lifting your lower legs away from the horse's sides in trot makes you aware of the lack of contact with your calves.

Closing your legs around your horse's body creates a secure contact with the seat and legs.

Upper body posture and arm movement

To focus on your upper body, you should think of being tall through your whole spine, with your shoulder-blades pressed down and back, keeping your chest open and your ribs lifted. If your core muscles are supporting you correctly, your shoulders should naturally be level, not one higher than the other, and they should be square to your hips. If your shoulders are correct, your upper arms will hang down by your sides, with your elbows lightly touching your body. Your elbows should be bent to give a straight line along the rein to the bit.

The purpose of the following exercises is to help maintain your upper body position while doing different things with your arms.

Reins in one hand

Put your reins in your outside hand and let your inside arm hang down by your side. (As you are on a circle on the lunge, your inside arm is the one to the inside of the horse, and your outside arm is on the outside of the horse.) Keep your shoulders and hips turning with the horse on the circle. Your instructor can keep the circle large, so you only have to turn your upper body slightly, or they can decrease the size of the circle so you have to turn more. The size of the circle should then be increased again. Try the same exercise with the inside hand in riding position, and practise keeping your hands parallel.

Ride with one hand on the reins, keeping your inside hand in riding position, and keeping your hands parallel.

Hands on hips

With the reins in your outside hand, place the other hand on your hip. Keep your shoulders back and down, and try not to lean in. Keep your weight on both seat bones, and your shoulders level. Repeat on the other rein with the other hand on your hip. Without the reins (have them knotted on the horse's

Left Riding with your inside hand on your hip can heighten your awareness of what your hips are doing. When riding on a circle, make sure your hips and shoulders are turning with the horse, and that you are looking forwards towards his ears.

Riding in trot with both hands on the hips. Feel how you hips move with the horse in each gait.

neck), place both hands on your hips. Feel how you hips move with the horse in each gait. Look forwards toward the horse's ears and turn your upper body without leaning in – keeping weight evenly on both seat bones.

Keeping your hands parallel

Riding without reins, with them knotted on the horse's neck as above, hold your hands in riding position. Try to keep them still all the time. This is not easy! Your arm joints have to act as shock-absorbers in order for your hands to remain still. This teaches you to keep the bit steady in the horse's mouth.

Riding without reins, keeping the hands parallel in riding position.

Arms behind your back

Without reins, place your inside arm across the small of your back. This helps to keep your shoulder-blade back and down and is a reminder to turn your shoulders with the horse. If you feel confident with this, place both arms behind your back. As well as improving your shoulder position, lifting your ribs and opening your chest, this exercise helps you to become more aware of your core muscles around your middle. Making transitions with your arms behind your back is a good test of how you are using your back and leg aids.

Above left Ride with your inside arm across the small of your back to keep your shoulder-blade back and down.

Above right Me on Norman with both arms behind my back.

Right Making transitions with the arms behind your back is a good test of your back and leg aids.

Hand exercises

The purpose of these exercises is to teach you to maintain a softly closed fist without 'fixing' the hands in place, by moving the hands out of position, then replacing them where they should be. This helps you to learn how to maintain a steady contact, not altering the tension along the rein. All you should feel is the connection of the reins between your hands and the bit (or the side rings on the lunge cavesson if the reins are attached to these instead of the bit).

Clench and relax the fists

This can be done without the reins at first, then with them. With your hands in riding position, clench the fists, and feel how tight this makes your forearms and shoulders. Relax them, so they are softly closed. Close your thumbs on to your first fingers. This will hold the rein contact.

With your hands in riding position, without holding the reins, close your fists softly.

Mind exercises

Riding on the lunge gives you time to focus on yourself. Quite often in daily life it is difficult to have any 'me time' at all, and if your riding lesson is the only time you have to yourself, you can become quite emotional, not necessarily about your riding or your horse, but other factors in your life that affect the way you feel and how you react to your horse, or respond to instruction from your teacher.

Riding horses can bring out all manner of emotions in riders. They can, for example, feel mortified that they did not realize that their own tension, anger, or stress affected their horse detrimentally, perhaps until their horse developed physical problems such as muscle wastage, tension in the back or neck, or 'bridle lameness' resulting from the rider hanging on to the contact on one rein over a period of time. Stress in other aspects of a rider's life can manifest itself during a lesson, particularly when, on the lunge, the rider has more 'thinking time'. Everyone is so busy these days, that time to yourself is a rare thing, so simply having time to focus on yourself riding your horse can be a real blessing and a pleasure, but can also be a counselling session in which your horse, and the instructor, can open a 'can of worms'. This is why it is so important that the instructor has empathy and the understanding to cope should the rider become emotional.

You may find that you become stressed and tense, and hold your breath as a result. Try to breathe as deeply and slowly as you can. If you are tense, and hold your breath, your horse will certainly pick up on this, and may well become tense himself as a result.

You should ride with energy. This does not mean being as active as possible on the horse, and fidgeting about, but drawing on your own bodily energy to give you strength, focus and effectiveness.

Remain focused on what you *want your horse to do* rather than what he *might do*. Many riders suffer from the 'what if' syndrome: 'What if my horse charges off?' 'What if my horse bucks?' 'What if I fall off?' Focusing on what you *want* to achieve clears your mind of useless 'chatter', which confuses the horse, who ends up reacting as you imagine he will. The moral of this is to think only what you want your horse to think, and don't give him any ideas about bucking, rearing, etc!

Your instructor should be observant enough to notice if you are becoming pale with anxiety, sweating or looking glazed, and bring the horse to a halt so you can compose yourself.

The lesson should end on a good note, when you feel a sense of achievement, and should not go on for so long that you cannot concentrate any longer, or feel physically tired. In this respect, whether teaching on or off the lunge, and with regard to either pupil or horse, an instructor should have the confidence to say 'Let's end on a good note' and the pupil should respect that decision. It can be very off-putting for an instructor if the pupil is constantly looking at their watch to make sure they get their 'money's worth'! Value should be put on the skill of the instructor and the sense of achievement that the pupil feels, rather than the precise duration of the lesson. Going on for another five minutes because 'it's not twelve o'clock yet', and having things unravel through tiredness, is a self-defeating error that is best avoided.

Above all, training with your horse should be fun!

Conclusion

I hope you have enjoyed reading this book, and that it will encourage you to use lungeing, long-reining and in-hand work in your horse's schooling. You will reach a new level of understanding with your horse, build trust between you, and generally have a lot of fun as well as improving his athletic ability. Happy groundwork!

Claire

OTHER BOOKS BY CLAIRE LILLEY

PUBLISHED BY J.A. ALLEN

200+ School Exercises with Poles

Dressage to Music

Stop, Go, Turn –
Perfecting the Basics of Riding

The Scales of Training Workbook